A Short Guide to the New Grammar

A Short Guide to the New Grammar

Jane Ervin
University of California, Los Angeles

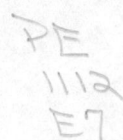

tb

Tinnon-Brown, Inc., *Book Publishers*
10835 Santa Monica Boulevard
Los Angeles, California 90025

Copyright © by Tinnon Brown, Inc. Printed in the United States of America. All rights reserved. This book, or parts thereof, may not be reproduced in any form without permission of the publisher.

SBN Number: 87252-008-0
LC Number: 68-28174

To the Master

Foreword

The New Grammar is still in the stages of evolution. Many questions remain unresolved. For example, there are still controversies concerning the best ways to explain such things as the tenses of verbs and the use of pronouns. Nevertheless, linguists have made great headway during the last few years in simplifying the description of our language. It is hoped that this short book—which avoids complicated explanations of the controversies—will help you to understand the new way of describing our language and will enable you to help your students to understand it.

Preface

This book is intended to be a short guide to the New Grammar for teachers of English at all levels. It describes its content, explains its derivation, and gives suggestions as to how it can be taught. In short, it answers three basic questions:

>What is the New Grammar?
>Where has it come from?
>How do you teach it?

The book begins by answering the second question: Where has it come from? The Introduction explains the earlier grammars, showing how each one has contributed to the New Grammar. This section not only sets the New Grammar in its proper perspective, but it also, hopefully, offers encouragement to those teachers who have been brought up on the earlier grammars and are hesitant to teach the new.

Part I answers the first question: What is the New Grammar? It describes the content of the New Grammar, analyzing the English language in terms of its structure, function, form, and sound.

Part II answers the third question: How do you teach it? It explains the use of the inductive approach and provides suggestions concerning different methods for teaching the New Grammar.

Unlike the earlier grammars, the New Grammar is not difficult to teach because it is based on a series of logical progressions, one concept following another in a clearly definable sequence. The teacher begins with the simplest sentence patterns and gradually builds upon them until the students have learned to deal with the most complex and complicated structures. Words are identified within the sentences by means of their functions and forms. The students are led to an understanding of the general concepts of grammar through functional descriptions rather than memorized definitions and through their own observations of the characteristics of the language.

JANE ERVIN

Los Angeles, California
November, 1968

Contents

INTRODUCTION: The Changing Concepts of the English Language

    Traditional Grammar   1
    Historical Grammar   4
    Structural Grammar   5
    New Grammar   8

PART I: An Analysis of the Structure of the English Language

Chapter 1   Basic Structural Patterns

    The Kernel Sentences   19
    Transforming the Kernel Sentences   25
    Punctuation: the Mechanics of Sentence Structure   40

Chapter 2   The Functions of Words

    The Word Classes   47
    The Functions of Content Words   56
    The Functions of Function Words   71

Chapter 3   The Forms of Words

    The Characteristics of Words   82
    The Forms of the Word Classes   83
    The Formation of Words   112

Chapter 4   **The Relationships of Sound to Meaning, Spelling, and Pronunciation**

      Phonemes and Graphemes:
      The Symbols of Language   122
      Structural Characteristics as Aids to Spelling and Pronunciation   125

PART II: A New Method for Teaching the English Language

Chapter 5   **The Inductive Method**

      The Inductive Method   134
      The Sequential Approach   137
      The "Janglish" Approach   152

Chapter 6   **The Relationships of Grammar to Literature, Writing, and Usage**

      Relating the New Grammar to Literature   159
      Relating the New Grammar to Writing   162
      Relating the New Grammar to Usage   164

Index   165

Introduction
The Changing Concepts of the English Language

> "Grammarians dispute and the case is still before the courts."
> —Horace, *Ars Poetica*

Four Basic Grammars: A Perspective

The English language has been interpreted in many different ways over the years. In this section, we will discuss the three major earlier grammars—traditional grammar, historical grammar, and structural grammar—and then give you a brief introduction to the New Grammar.

A review of the changing concepts of the English language is important for several reasons. First, it will help you to understand how the New Grammar developed, because each of the earlier grammars has contributed to it in some way. Second, it will introduce you to the different grammatical concepts currently being taught in our schools, because research indicates that all of these grammars are being taught. Third, it will help you to introduce the New Grammar to those students who have learned the earlier grammars, because you will understand the kinds of concepts they were taught and how these concepts were presented.

Traditional Grammar

This approach introduces the English language as an intricate structure involving a highly complicated pattern of rules and definitions that must be memorized by students. Based upon Latin and developed by grammarians in the eighteenth century, traditional grammar is essentially a description of the language. It offers no particular theory. There are many inconsistencies and students usually find its explanations difficult to comprehend.

The rationale behind traditional grammar is that there is an "ideal" or "correct" language that can be articulated and explained by a series of definitions. Once the student learns these definitions, he presumably has complete command of English. Unfortunately, however, this is not quite the case because the definitions are often subjective and inconclusive. This is seen, for example, in the vague description of a sentence as "a group of words expressing a complete thought," which provides no real criterion for deciding whether a group of words constitutes a sentence or not. It is also seen in the definition of a direct object of a verb as "answering the question when? or what?"

Traditional definitions abound in arbitrary classifications, such as those dealing with the eight parts of speech (noun, verb, adjective, adverb, pronoun, conjunction, preposition, and interjection). A noun, for example, is categorically defined as "the name of a person, place, or thing" while a verb is "a word that expresses action or a state of being." Like the definition of a sentence, these definitions are untenable because they either apply to only a limited set of data (as in the case of the noun definition) or are so broad as to be meaningless (as in the case of the verb definition). Not all nouns are persons, places or things for many express action (such as "suspect"), and if we accepted the verb definition we should have to describe such words as "action," "operation," and "arrival" as verbs.

Still another problem with the traditional definitions is that they shift direction. By this we mean that they mix the two levels upon which the English language can be described: the word class level and the relational level. The definition of a noun, for example, tells what it is (the name of a person, place or thing) while the definition of an adjective tells what it does (modifies a noun). In the definition of an adjective we again meet the problem of overgeneralization for it groups together quite different structures and classes, such as "our mother," "working mother," "harassed mother" and "mother outside." Admittedly the traditional grammarians try to overcome this by using such terms as "limiting adjective," "descriptive adjective," "participle," and "gerund," but these are clumsy and clearly contradict other definitions.

A weakness of traditional grammar, which is also found in structural grammar, is the number of conflicting descriptions, rules, and definitions. For example, some traditionalists define eight parts of speech, while others define only seven (omitting the interjection); some present purely semantic definitions ("a noun is the name of a person, place or thing"); others attempt a functional definition ("a noun is a word that names something"); while still others combine the two types ("a noun is a word used to name a person, place or thing"). Confusion also exists about pronouns. Some cite four kinds, others six, and others even as many as twelve.

Traditional grammarians believe that the *word* is the most important element of communication. Thus sentences are broken down and analyzed in terms of parts of speech, and the relationship that each part of speech has to the other words in a sentence. Sometimes sentences are analyzed by means of a diagram. Various methods are used for diagraming: some involve left-slanting lines, some right-slanting lines, some perpendicular lines, and some dashed lines. The most typical method is the one illustrated below; it diagrams the sentence, "The pretty girl came into the room."

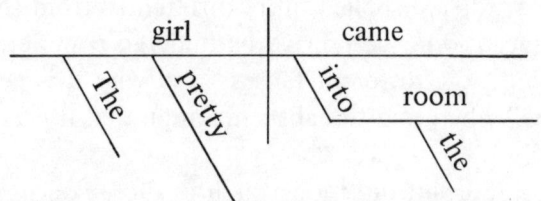

In summary, the traditional grammarians believe there exists an "ideal" or "correct" language. Their approach to the acquisition of this ideal language is purely subjective, inconclusive and often self-conflicting. Yet, although the traditional grammarians fail to explain fully the basic structure of the English language, they have made a great contribution in providing us with a useful terminology. Admittedly we use this terminology in rather a different way today, but at least it has given us a starting point.

Historical Grammar

During the late nineteenth and early twentieth centuries a group of philologists, of whom the Dane Otto Jesperson [1914] was the most famous, sought a new way to explain the intricacies and apparent irregularities of English. Turning to history, these historical grammarians first observed that word forms change gradually over the years. They then proceeded to challenge the traditionalists' concept of an ideal language based on Latin by illustrating that Latin itself had undergone many changes and developments over the years and thus presented no one form that could be called "ideal."

The historical grammarians also observed that there exist certain similarities between words of quite different languages, and from this they developed the concept of language "families." For example, they maintained that English, together with German, Dutch, and the Scandinavian tongues, came from the "parent" language, Indo-European. By noting these similarities, the historical grammarians brought answers to many of the unsolved problems concerning the irregularities of English. They explained why many words are spelled quite differently from the way they are pronounced; why certain verbs undergo complete changes in structure to denote different tenses; and why it is permissible to say "it is me" when traditionalists maintain that it is mandatory to say "it is I."

Other important questions, such as those concerning the presence of plurality in our language and its regularity of formation, were answered for us by the historical grammarians. They illustrated, for example, that all nouns (with the exception of a very few, such as "chaos") have a means of incorporating plurality and that they acquire plurality regularly (again with a few exceptions) either by adding an *s* (or its spelling variant *es*) to the end of a word or by mutation (the changing of a vowel). They even showed that mutation is regular by pointing out that the singular vowel sound made in the center or back of the mouth is always replaced by a vowel formed in the front of the mouth. Thus "tooth" becomes "teeth," "man" becomes "men," and "foot" becomes "feet."

Structural Grammar

The historical grammarians' research in the changing forms of language, together with the results of certain studies that showed little relationship between the knowledge of grammar and the ability to write, brought an increased interest in the structure and formation of the English language and a discontent with the prescriptive nature of formal grammar. Thus, in the early part of this century, a group of linguists, of whom Leonard, Fries, and Sledd are the most famous, sought an entirely new way to explain our language. Turning their attention to the language of the day, and particularly to spoken language, they devised a method of analyzing language in terms of different levels. Called "syntactic levels," they are based on speech sounds and their meanings.

The first level deals with the basic sounds of language, called "phonemes," which differentiate meaning. For example, the sound of *d* in "dog" and of *l* in "log" are phonemes because the words contrast only in these two sounds yet have two entirely different meanings. There are approximately 40 of these elemental sounds, which are represented in writing by a limited alphabet of 26 letters or "graphemes."

The second, and higher, level deals with the smallest units of meaning, called "morphemes," which come from the regular combinations of phonemes. The word "cat" is a morpheme, being formed from the phonemes *c-a-t*. There are two kinds of morphemes: "bound" and "free." "Cat" is a free morpheme because it can stand by itself in a sentence. On the other hand, "trans" is a bound morpheme because it cannot stand by itself but must be joined by a free morpheme. The third level deals with "phrase structure," which comes from the combination of morphemes; consisting of groups of words, this level involves more complex meanings.

The main concept underlying structural grammar is that language goes from form to meaning rather than from meaning to form as in traditional grammar. That is, the meaning of a word, sentence, or any component of language is determined by, and dependent upon, its form and structure. Thus, words are defined by describing and identifying their structural characteristics, such as inflectional endings (*-s, -ed*), derivational endings (*-ness, -ation*), and characteristic suffixes (*-age, -ism*). In structural grammar, then, a noun is recognized by its ability to indicate plurality (adding *-s* or *-es*), to indicate possession (*-'s, -s'*), and by certain characteristic suffixes (*-ness, -ist*) rather than by the knowledge that it is the name of a person, place, or thing.

The structural linguists defined only four parts of speech, in contrast to the traditional eight. Instead of referring to nouns, verbs, adjectives, and adverbs, they discussed Class I, Class II, Class III, and Class IV words. They grouped all other words into a class called "function words," of which they isolated 15 to 17 groups.

The structural linguists were interested in more than the mere identification of word classes. They were also interested in the way words function. They observed how words are put together to form phrases and clauses and how almost everything in the English language depends upon specific word order.

The principal aim of the structural linguists was to bring about a clearer understanding of the English language by describing it in simple, concise, and complete terms. Unfortunately, however, their terminology became so extensive and so cumbrous to define that even the most adaptable teachers have found it difficult to comprehend and even more difficult to teach. Also, like the traditional definitions they so despised, many of their definitions have proven inadequate.

For example, the structural linguists' definition of a noun as being a word that forms its plural by adding -*s* does not account for such words as "chaos." Their description of an adjective as being a word that adds the endings -*er* and -*est* (as in "bright," "brighter," and "brightest") requires putting "beautiful," "courageous," and "hopeful" in a different class from "pretty," "old," and "sad," and defining the word "tear" as an adjective ("tear," "terror," "terraced"). Their premise that words function in particular places within groups fails to explain such things as the difference between "the man was seated by the door" and "the girl was pulled by the boy." Nor does it explain whether the word "black" in "it is black" is a noun or an adjective. Another weakness in structural grammar is that it cannot explain the relationship between the active and the passive voice.

In contrast to the traditional concept that "correct" or "good" English is rigidly defined by rules of syntax and logic, the structural linguists maintained that it is set by the standards and usage of the time. They did not consider "anything" acceptable, as many people contend, but acknowledged that the common usage of a community is correct for that community.

The structuralists maintained that the most important purpose of language is the effective communication of a message; thus "good" English is any language that, as Krapp says, "hits its mark."* Rather than learning rules for the avoidance of "errors" as in traditional grammar, students are helped in acquiring effective expression through *observation* of the varying requirements of language and practice, and in adapting language to a variety of situations. But the lack of any clear or acceptable pattern of language in structural grammar makes the teacher's task difficult and burdensome. He has to be particularly sensitive to the different levels of language and the functional varieties of usage, as well as to the language customs of the local community and changes in language usage generally.

---

* George Philip Krapp, *Modern English* (New York: Charles Scribners' Sons, 1909), p. 332.

In summary, the structural linguists brought about a greater awareness of the structure and formation of our language and developed the concept that language goes from form to meaning, in contrast to the traditionalists' belief that it goes from meaning to form. They were unable, however, to produce any foolproof descriptions of the intricacies of our language or to come to grips with the essential nature of English and language learning.

New Grammar

The New Grammar, which is also called "transformational grammar," "generative grammar," and "the New English," was developed to eliminate the errors and shortcomings of the earlier grammars and, at the same time, to incorporate the best aspects of each one. It was first introduced in the 1950's, mainly through a book called *Syntactic Structures* (Hague, 1957) written by Noam Chomsky, the chief linguist in the development of the new approach.

The unique feature of the New Grammar is its *focus on the sentence.* This is seen in Chomsky's definition of grammar, which states that "grammar is a device for generating the sentences of language" (p. 45). Chomsky's basic concept is that there is a small group of sentences, called "kernel" sentences, that form the core or kernel of our language. A kernel sentence is "simple, active, declarative" with no complex noun or verb phrases. The sentence, "The girl is reading the book," is a kernel sentence.

The simplest kernel sentence of the New Grammar is very similar to the simple subject-verb-complement sentence of traditional grammar for it contains "a noun phrase plus a verb phrase." A "noun phrase" consists simply of a noun and usually an article or determiner. A "verb phrase" consists of a main verb and sometimes an auxiliary, plus an optional noun phrase that is very similar to the traditional complement. Thus, the simple kernel sentence = a noun phrase + a verb phrase (+ an optional noun phrase).

For example,

noun phrase	verb phrase	complement
Joan	baked	a cake.
John	came.	
The girl	ate	the cake.

There are five kernel sentences:

1. **noun-verb** — John came.
2. **noun-verb-noun** — Joan baked a cake.
3. **noun-linking verb-noun** — Joan is a girl.
4. **noun-linking verb-adjective** — Joan is unhappy.
5. (a) **noun-verb-noun-noun** — They elected John president.
   (b) **noun-verb-noun-adjective** — The girl painted the wall blue.

All other sentences are "generated from" (built upon) these kernel sentences. This is done by means of "transformations." Transformations occur through the introduction of new elements (such as adjectives and negatives) into a kernel sentence, as in the following example.

kernel sentence: The girl ate the cake.
kernel sentence transformed: The pretty girl ate the chocolate cake slowly.

Transformations also occur through the rearrangement of the elements of a sentence, as in an interrogative sentence ("Did the girl eat the cake?") or a passive sentence ("The cake was eaten by the girl.").

The advantage of this new approach to grammar is that it provides a simple method for the generation and understanding of the most complex and sophisticated sentence patterns. It is like structural grammar in that it defines the sentence in terms of its physical characteristics, but it also indicates the exact nature of such things as subordination and the relationship between a kernel sentence and a passive, negative, or interrogative sentence. The passive voice, for example, is explained as being merely the rearrangement of the essential elements of a kernel sentence with the addition of certain other elements. Thus the passive voice is formed by transferring the object of the sentence to the subject; by using the past participle of the verb (usually formed by adding the morpheme *-ed* or *-en*) and adding some form of the verb "to be"; and by adding the word "by." For example,

kernel sentence:	**subject**	**predicate**	**complement**
	He	has eaten	the cake.
the passive form:	The cake + has + been + eaten + by + the man.		

Because sentences are the key to the New Grammar, it is not surprising that words are identified by means of their positions and functions within sentences. Nouns and verbs are identified as the main words or "headwords" in noun and verb phrases; adjectives and adverbs are identified as "expanders" or "modifiers" of the headwords; and prepositional phrases, verbal phrases, etc. are called "word-group modifiers."

In traditional grammar, students are required to learn rules and definitions in order to understand sentences. In the New Grammar, students acquire this understanding by observing the language and discovering for themselves its fundamentals or rules. Thus, like the linguists who developed the New Grammar, they formulate their own definitions from what they observe. For example, they not only discover that certain kinds of words function in certain ways within sentences, they also learn that a variety of forms can appear in a given function. They observe, for example, that all classes of words can perform in the subject function.

The **blue** is prettier.   (adjective)

Today seems endless.	(adverb)
That **girl** is pretty.	(noun)
Shopping is tiring.	(verb)
These are mine.	(function word)

The New Grammar recognizes four main word classes, as in structural grammar, but returns to traditional grammar to name them: nouns, verbs, adjectives, and adverbs. (The New Grammar also retains traditional terms to describe other aspects of sentence patterns, such as the forms and tenses of verbs and the concept of direct and indirect objects.) All other words are "function words," which are subdivided into smaller groups according to particular functions (determiners, auxiliaries, connectives, intensifiers, and pronouns). Again as in structural grammar, the New Grammar identifies words as belonging to these classes by form and structure (such as inflectional endings, affixes, capitalization) as well as by position and function within sentences. Attention is thus paid to phonemes (the basic elements of sound and meaning) and morphemes (the smallest units of meaning) and the way words are constructed. At the same time, study of the historical development of words is incorporated into the New Grammar to explain many of the irregularities of word formation unaccounted for by structural analysis.

The New Grammar is also similar to structural grammar in that students learn to spell by recognizing the relationship of written communication to oral communication and by observing the relationship of sound and stress to spelling. On the other hand, the New Grammar is different from structural grammar in that it makes a distinction between spoken language and written language. Spoken language incorporates pitch, stress, juncture, and even gestures to convey its message, whereas written language relies almost solely upon its graphic symbols. It is because written language has no special reinforcements that the New Grammar emphasizes the importance of word order and the understanding of the fundamentals or rules intrinsic to the language.

In summary, the New Grammar concerns itself with the mastery of the sentence and the manipulation of its basic patterns. Students learn that there are certain fundamentals or rules inherent in the English language that must be followed in order to communicate their thoughts clearly, accurately, and concisely. They discover these fundamentals by observing language, by forming generalized rules or principles based upon their observations, and by relating these generalizations to the understanding of specific facts. In other words, to a large extent, they repeat the process employed by the linguists who developed the New Grammar.

In order to teach the New Grammar, a teacher should be knowledgeable about:

the basic structure of the language—in order to teach kernel sentences and their transformations;
the form and function of words—in order to teach word meaning;
phonemics—in order to teach spelling, reading, and sentence construction;
the history of the English language—in order to teach the complexities of spelling and word structure;
usage and language levels—in order to teach the essential differences between spoken and written language;
rhetoric—in order to teach students how to develop their styles of writing.

At the same time, the "new" English teacher must be able to teach through the inductive method so that students can be led to observe new and/or familiar data, to preceive common elements, to make statements of generalization, and to see relationships.

As this Introduction has pointed out, the New Grammar is not really so very new. It combines in one approach all the best aspects of the three earlier grammars with several new concepts in order to present the English language more clearly, simply, and comprehensively. The charts that follow show the relationships among the four grammars that we have discussed. The first chart shows the differences and similarities among the grammars; the second chart shows the contributions that traditional grammar, historical grammar, and structural grammar have made to the New Grammar.

Chart I: A Comparison of Grammars

	Traditional Grammar	Structural Grammar	New Grammar
Method	*Deductive:* Students learn rules and definitions and apply them to an analysis of the language. Rules are memorized and then applied. The approach is intellectual.	*Inductive:* Students are led to observe, use, and make language. Learning is acquired through discovery and manipulation of the language. The approach is practical.	*Inductive:* Students learn by discovery, observing the structure of the language and relating generalizations to an understanding of specific fact. The approach combines practicality with intellectualism.
Basic Concepts	(1) There is an "ideal" or "correct" language based on Latin and rigidly defined by rules of syntax and logic.	There is no "ideal" or "correct" language. Correctness rests upon usage within the community.	There is a correct form of written language. Spoken language is correct according to the conventions of the situation and the times.
	(2) English grammar is permanent and changeless; historical change is ignored.	Language is constantly changing; change is normal; it does not represent corruption but improvement.	Spoken language changes with the times.
	(3) Written language is different from spoken language.	Written language is a repetition of spoken language.	Written language is different from spoken language.
	(4) Emphasis is upon rhetoric.	Emphasis is upon oral communication.	Emphasis is upon rhetoric.
	(5) Language goes from meaning to form.	Language goes from form to meaning.	Language goes from form to meaning.

	(6) The *word* is the most important element of communication.	*Word order* gives meaning to language.	The *sentence* is the basic means of communication.
Definitions	Definitions play a key part; they are semantic, inconclusive, and often conflicting; they also mix levels (e.g., the definition of a noun tells what it is while the definition of an adjective tells what it does).	No definitions; the structure of English is merely described and observed. However, there is an extensive terminology that tends to be difficult to follow and is often inadequate.	Definitions are avoided; students are led to observe the language and to develop and apply their own generalizations. However, there are definite rules which must be obeyed in order to communicate effectively.
Analysis of the Language	Language is described rather than analyzed.	Language is analyzed in terms of syntactic levels based on speech sounds and meaning. There are three levels: (1) phonemes—the elemental sounds and meanings of language, such as *e, a, t.* (2) morphemes—the smallest units of meaning, such as "cat," "dog." (3) phrase structure—the combination of morphemes to form groups of words.	Language is analyzed in terms of its physical characteristics, intonation, and word order. Emphasis is put upon the structure of the sentence. There are five basic or kernel sentences which form the core of the English language. All other sentences are developed from these: (1) noun-verb (2) noun-verb-noun (3) noun-linking verb-noun (4) Noun-linking verb-adjective (5) (a) noun-verb-noun-noun (b) noun-verb-noun-adjective

Chart I: A Comparison of Grammars (continued)

	Traditional Grammar	Structural Grammar	New Grammar

The Sentence	The word is the most important element of communication. Sentences are broken down and analyzed in terms of parts of speech, showing the relationship of each to the others. The sentence is usually analyzed by means of a diagram.	Little attention is paid to the sentence as such. The focus is upon word groups and how meaning is conveyed by the positioning of words within a group.	The sentence is analyzed in terms of its subject-predicate structure. For example,
			
			 The pretty girl / came into the room.
			
			 It is also divided into noun and verb phrases, which consist of headwords (the noun or the verb) and their determiners and modifiers (individual words or groups of words). For example,
			   headword: girl
			   modifier: pretty
			   determiner: the
			
			   headword: came
			   modifier: into the room

The following diagram illustrates the sentence, "The pretty girl came into the room.":

```
   girl  |  came  \ into \ room
   ------|---------\------\-----
    \ The \ pretty          \ the
```

Basic Structural Patterns

	Traditional Grammar	Structural Grammar	New Grammar
Words	Words are arbitrarily classified into eight parts of speech: nouns, verbs, adjectives, adverbs, pronouns, prepositions, conjunctions, and interjections.	Words are grouped into four main classes called Class I, Class II, Class III, Class IV. All other words are called function words, of which there are 15-17 groups.	Words are grouped into four main classes: nouns, verbs, adjectives, and adverbs. All other words are called function words.
	Parts of speech are presented as functional elements. The subject and object are rigidly identified as the noun function. Prepositions and conjunctions are connectives. A pronoun takes the place (or function) of a noun.	Words are classified in terms of: (1) structure—by their inflectional endings (-s, -ed); derivational endings (-ness, -ation); affixes, capitalization, etc. (2) position—by their positions within a group of words. (3) relationship—by their relationships to the other words within the group.	Words are identified by means of their forms and functions and by their historical development. Students discover that certain kinds of words function in certain ways within a sentence and that a variety of different forms can appear in a given function.

Chart II: Contributions to the New Grammar

Traditional Grammar	Historical Grammar	Structural Grammar
Initiated the idea of explaining the relationships among the varying structures of our language.	Initiated the idea that a greater understanding of English is acquired through the study of its history.	Initiated the idea that language goes from form to meaning.
Provided a useful terminology: noun, verb, adverb, subject, predicate, etc.		Analyzed language in terms of its physical characteristics and syntactical levels, and emphasized word order.
Emphasized the difference between written and spoken language.		Initiated an inductive approach to learning grammar. Students observe language and through their own reasoning arrive at generalizations which they can apply to a better understanding of English.
Emphasized rhetoric.		Identified four main word classes and grouped all other words as function words.
		Identified words by their structure, position, and function.

Part One | An Analysis of the Structure of the English Language

Chapter One
Basic Structural Patterns

The Kernel Sentences

People who speak English can use a variety of words to communicate their ideas and feelings, but in order to communicate effectively they must arrange the words they select in a particular order. For example, if a man stopped you in the street and said, "Is time the what," you would have no idea what he was trying to say to you. But if he said, "What is the time?" you would promptly look at your watch and tell him the time of day.

Notice how word order is important in conveying meaning in these two examples.

> The cat chased the dog.
> The dog chased the cat.

It is the discovery of the importance of this innate word order in our language that has enabled linguists to formulate the fundamentals or "rules" of the New Grammar.

The most important fundamental of the New Grammar is that word order in English forms definite structural patterns. These structural patterns are sentences, our basic units of communication. There are five basic or *kernel* sentence patterns that form the kernel or core of our language; they may be expanded or transformed into an infinite variety of other sentences, capable of expressing the most complicated ideas.

Elements of the Kernel Sentence

The simplest kernel sentence of the English language, from which all other sentences may be developed, consists of **a subject** and a **predicate**. The subject precedes the predicate.

The **subject** usually consists of a *noun phrase*. This can be a single noun or a group of words "clustered" or grouped around a noun. The noun is called the *headword* of the noun phrase.

The **predicate** consists of a *verb phrase*. This can be a single verb, or it can be a verb followed by a group of words that completes its sense called the *complement* or "completer." (The last term is used mainly by Roberts.)* The verb is called the *headword* of the verb phrase.

Headwords are identified in the following sentences, nouns by solid lines, verbs by broken lines, to illustrate subject-predicate structure.

> John / came.
> The pretty girl / sailed into the room.
> John / followed Mary.
> John and Mary / crossed the road.

Notice how "into the room," "Mary," and "the road" are complements. They supplement verbs that do not express by themselves all that a writer wishes to say. Or, to put it another way, they answer the questions "where?" "who?" or "what?"

In summary, the basic structure of a sentence may be visualized as **subject + predicate (+ complement)**, or as *noun phrase + verb phrase*. The subject precedes the predicate, and the headword of the subject is usually a noun. The headword of the predicate is always a verb.

The Five Kernel Sentence Patterns

Pattern 1.
The most elementary sentence pattern in the English language is the basic noun-verb structure, usually indicated by the notation N-V. The verb in this pattern is called an *intransitive or predicate verb* because it can function as both verb and complement. That is, it does not need a complement to complete its sense because

---

* Paul Roberts, *The Roberts English Series: A Linguistics Program* (New York: Harcourt, Brace & World, Inc., 1967).

it answers the questions "who?" "what?" and "where?"

noun	verb
Every shop	was closed.
John	came.
The clouds	were gathering ominously.

Notice that "ominously" in the last sentence is not a complement because, although it may make the sentence more expressive, it is not essential to its meaning.

Pattern 2.
The second sentence pattern consists of the noun-verb structure plus a complement. In this case, the verb is called a *transitive verb* because it needs a complement to complete its sense. This pattern is indicated by N-V-N because the complement always consists of another noun phrase. When a noun phrase appears after the verb it is called the *direct object.*

noun	verb	noun
The suspicious man	put	the papers into his pocket.
Mother	baked	a cake.
The yachtsman	fought	the storm bravely.
We	lost	our way.

The term transitive means "to pass over to" or "to go across." Thus a verb taking a direct object (as in the N-V-N pattern of Pattern 2 or the N-V-N-N pattern of Pattern 5) is a transitive verb because the action stated by the verb passes over to the receiver of the action. For example, in the sentence "John hit Mary," the verb "hit" is transitive because the action of "hitting" is passed over to Mary. The verb is still called transitive when the action is expressed passively ("Mary was hit by John"), because, although Mary is now the subject of the verb, she is still affected by its action. When a transitive verb is used passively, it does not have a direct object because the object has become the subject.

Intransitive verbs do not have objects. There are two kinds of intransitive verbs: (1) the "complete" intransitive verb or "predicate verb" (as in the simple N-V pattern of Pattern 1), which does not need an object because the verb is complete in itself; and (2) the "linking verb" (as in the N-LV-N pattern of Pattern 3), which does not have an object because the complement refers back to the subject of the verb.

A verb may be transitive or intransitive according to the sentence pattern in which it is used. For example,

John **is cleaning** his new car. (N-V-N pattern, verb used transitively)
John **is cleaning** today. (N-V pattern, verb used intransitively)

Pattern 3.
The third pattern, indicated by the notation N-LV-N, is similar to the second pattern except that the subject noun and predicate noun are joined by what is called a *linking verb*. Linking verbs include forms of "to be," "to seem," "to appear," "to look," "to taste," "to smell," and "to become"—Roberts refers to them as "seem" verbs. The complements of linking verbs always refer back to the subject and are called *linking-verb complements*.

noun	linking verb	noun
The football team	looked	a motley group.
My father	was	the mayor of our town.
France	is	a country.

Pattern 4.
This pattern is formed when an adjective follows a linking verb. Like the predicate noun in the third pattern, the adjective relates back to (tells more of) the subject noun. The notation for this pattern is N-LV-A.

noun	linking verb	adjective
The apple pie	tasted	good.
Joan	seemed	discontented.
His uniform	was	immaculate.

Pattern 5.
The fifth pattern contains two complements, an *inner complement* and an *outer complement.* As might be expected, these terms describe the positions of the complements. If the outer complement is the *direct object,* the inner complement is called the *indirect object.* Both the direct and indirect object add to the meaning, or sense, of the verb, but whereas the direct object is essential in completing its sense, the indirect object is not.

noun	verb	noun	noun
The mother	gave	her screaming daughter	the toy.
Lynn	passed	her brother	the piece of cake.
I	told	my friend	a secret.

An indirect object can be identified by the signal words "to" or "for," which may or may not actually appear in the phrase. Thus "her screaming daughter" in the first sentence is an indirect object because the mother gave *to* her screaming daughter the toy. "The toy" could not be the indirect object because the sentence would not make sense if "to" were added before it.

If the direct object is the inner complement, the outer complement is called the *objective complement.* The objective complement is called this because it relates to the direct object and is complementary to it.

noun	verb	noun	noun
The team	elected	John Smith	their captain.
Sally	considers	David	her boyfriend.
Stan	thinks	his wife	a heroine.

Sometimes an adjective functions as an objective complement.

noun	verb	noun	adjective
The little girl	painted	her picture	green.
The class	called	him	dishonest.

Pattern 5 therefore has three variations: (1) noun-verb-noun-noun, with the inner noun phrase functioning as an indirect object, the outer as a direct object; (2) noun-verb-noun-noun, with the inner noun phrase functioning as a direct object, the outer as an objective complement; and (3) noun-verb-noun-adjective, with the inner noun phrase functioning as a direct object, the adjective as an objective complement. Despite the difference in functions, the basic form of the first two is the same and they are both noted as (a) N-V-N-N, while the third is noted as (b) N-V-N-A.

The Uses of Sentences

Sentences are used for four purposes: (1) to make statements or present facts, (2) to command or request, (3) to exclaim, and (4) to ask questions.

To Make Statements or Present Facts

All of the basic or kernel sentences fall into this category. For example, the sentence, "There are three pairs of shoes in the closet that need repairing," gives facts; the sentence, "I want to watch that television program," makes a statement.

To Command or Request

Command or request sentences are used to command, request, or direct. The subject is always "you," although usually the "you" is implied rather than actually included in the sentence. Patterns 1, 2, and 5 may be used as command sentences. For example,

(You) come here.	(N-V)
(You) please leave me.	(N-V-N)
(You) give your brother a piece of cake.	(N-V-N-N)
(You) paint the clouds grey.	(N-V-N-A)

To Exclaim

Exclamatory sentences express surprise or strong emotion. Sometimes they are complete sentence patterns, but more often they are fragments that have become acceptable means of expression. They are always followed by an exclamation mark.

Good Heavens!
What a temperature!
It's freezing!
My goodness!
Oh!
Ouch!

To Ask Questions
Question sentences are formed by the rearrangement of kernel sentence patterns by means of transformations—the topic of the next section. They may also be formed by beginning the sentence with such words as "when," "whenever," "what," "whatever," "where," "wherever," "which," "whichever," "who," "whoever," "whom," "whomever," "whose," "why," "how." Question sentences always end with a question mark.

Are you going home now?
When shall we leave?
Whatever made you do that?
Which one do you want?

Transforming the Kernel Sentences

The five kernel sentences are the basic units of communication in our language. All other sentences are "generated from" them, or built upon them, by means of *transformations.* Transformations are made in two ways: (1) by the *rearrangement* of the elements of a kernel sentence, and (2) by the *introduction* of new elements into a kernel sentence.

Rearranging the Elements of a Kernel Sentence

A kernel sentence may be transformed through the rearrangement of its elements in order to ask a question, or in order to make a statement in the passive voice.

To Ask a Question

The usual pattern of a kernel sentence is subject-predicate-complement. However, when we want to ask a question, we change this order and replace the period at the end of the sentence with a question mark.

normal pattern:	subject	predicate	complement
	You	have	a dog.
	The roses	are	dead.

inverted pattern to form a question:

	predicate	subject	complement
	Have	you	a dog?
	Are	the roses	dead?

The simplest inversion occurs with the verbs "to have" and "to be." Other verbs require the addition of a type of function word known as an *auxiliary verb* to complete the inversion. An auxiliary verb is a "helping" verb which is attached to a main verb, serving either as a signal for the verb or as an indication of a subtle change in its meaning, particularly in regard to time, intent, feeling, or condition. For example,

>You **can** go home now.
>I **may** go out this evening.
>I **could have** gone out this morning.

Auxiliaries act as modifiers of the main verbs; they add to the meaning of the verb to which they are attached and have meaning only in relation to that verb. Exceptions to this are forms of "to be," "to have," "to get," "to keep," and "to do," which can function as main verbs. The principal auxiliaries:

am, is, are, was, were	can, could
do, does, did	get, gets, got
going to	have, has, had
keep, keeps, kept	may, might
must	ought to
shall, should	used to
will, would	

In an inversion involving the addition of an auxiliary, the subject is put between the auxiliary and the verb. For example,

normal pattern:	subject	predicate	complement
	You	like	tea.
	They	enjoyed	the party.

inverted pattern to form a question:

auxiliary	subject	predicate	complement
Do	you	like	tea?
Did	they	enjoy	the party?

Both types of inversions can be answered by a definite "yes" or "no." But this is not possible for all the questions we wish to ask. The kind of question that cannot be answered so simply is often called a "wh" question because it is usually introduced by a word beginning with "wh"—"when," "whenever"; "what," "whatever"; "where," "wherever"; "which," "whichever"; "who," "whoever"; "whom," "whomever"; "whose"; "why"—as well as one not beginning with "wh," "how." Once again, the subject-predicate order is reversed, and an auxiliary verb is added when the verb is not "to have" or "to be."

"wh" word	auxiliary	subject	predicate	complement
When	are	you	leaving?	
Where	has	the cat	gone?	
How	will	I	find	the house?

Sometimes the order is not changed in making a question. This happens when the word "who" is used ("Who wants some lunch?"), or in such cases as

How many girls are going to the party?
What games are being planned for the party?
Which styles are in fashion?

This inconsistency in the formation of questions comes from the fact that many phrases have been condensed for easier and faster spoken communication and have gradually become part of our written language. Sometimes, in asking a question verbally, we do not invert the sentence or use a "wh" word, but instead rely wholly upon intonation and change of pitch and stress to imply that we want an answer: "The girls are going to the party?"

To Indicate the Passive

A kernel sentence may be transformed into a passive sentence by the rearrangement of its basic elements and by the addition of several elements. The object of the verb becomes the subject; the past participle of the verb (usually formed by adding the morpheme *-ed* or *-en*) is used with some form of the verb "to be"; and the verb is usually followed by a prepositional phrase beginning with the word "by" which takes the original subject as its object.

	subject	predicate	complement
normal pattern:	The man	has eaten	the cake.
passive form:	The cake + has + be+en + eaten + by + the man.		

Introducing New Elements into a Kernel Sentence

By introducing new elements into a kernel sentence, we may reverse the sentence's meaning, or we may expand its meaning.

To Reverse the Meaning of a Kernel Sentence

When we want to reverse the meaning of a sentence, we add the word "not" and call it a "negative sentence." The simplest negation occurs with the verb "to be."

> He is very clever.
> He is **not** very clever.

Other verbs require the addition of an auxiliary and a change in the verb formation to complete the negative. In these instances, "not" is put between the auxiliary and the verb.

He came home early.
He **did not come** home early.
The happy girls waved goodbye.
The happy girls **did not wave** goodbye.

To Expand the Meaning of a Kernel Sentence

The kernel sentences that form the core of our language can be expanded and developed to express highly complex thoughts and ideas in many colorful and interesting ways. Kernel sentences are expanded by the introduction of supplementary structures, which may be either individual words or groups of words. The structure of the basic sentence pattern is not changed—new elements are merely introduced. For example, see how the simple N-V-N pattern, "He explained it," can be developed.

He explained it clearly.	(expanded by a single word, an adverb)
He explained it with clarity.	(expanded by a group of words with no subject or predicate, an adverbial phrase)
He explained it so that it was clear.	(expanded by a group of words with a subject and predicate, an adverbial clause)
He explained it and I found that it was now clear to me.	(expanded by another separate and complete sentence pattern)

Expansion is accomplished by means of *modification.* Modifiers add exactness and precision to the words they are attached to. They enable us to communicate our ideas more fully and more colorfully. We saw examples of the use of modifiers in our earlier discussion of noun and verb phrases. For example, in the sentence "The pretty girl came into the room," "girl" is the headword of the noun phrase and "came" is the headword of the verb phrase. "Pretty" and "into the room" are modifiers because they tell us more about "girl" and "came." "The" is a function word, not a modifier, because it does not expand "girl" but merely helps us to identify the word as a noun.

In the following sentences, notice how the five kernel sentences are expanded without changing their basic patterns:

            N
1. Tim, the poor little lame boy in *A Christmas Carol*,
            V
died.

            N   V   N
2. The heavy rains completely washed out the road that

led into Yosemite Valley.

            N   LV   N
3. The hardy energetic rangers are expert tree fellers,

mountaineers, and geologists.
     N
4. The rivers, which had been overflowing when we were
                       LV   A
at Yosemite in the spring, were now almost dry.

                  N   V
5. (a) The weary, hot parents gave their even wearier
        N   N
children a cool drink.
      N   V
The people in favor of the new freeway consider
                      N   N
those enormous, centuries-old redwood trees a hazard.
          N   V   N
(b) The large furry black bears considered the tour-
  A
ists bothersome.

Modification can be used to expand the meanings of kernel sentences in two ways. First, individual words within a sentence may be modified. This is done through the introduction of single-word modifiers, such as adjectives and adverbs, and through the introduction of word-group modifiers, such as prepositional phrases, verbal phrases, subordinate clauses, and appositives. Second, an entire kernel sentence—the sentence as a whole—may be expanded through subordination, coordination, and the use of absolute structures.

Modifying Words Within Sentences
First, let us consider the ways in which individual words within a kernel sentence may be modified.

Single-word modifiers. The simplest expansion of kernel sentences occurs through the introduction of single-word modifiers.

Almost all of the language forms in English may be used to modify a noun, whether it is in the subject function or the complement function. The most usual modifier, however, is the adjective. Noun modifiers usually precede the noun or are placed very close to it. Several modifiers may be attached to the same noun.

In the following examples, single-word modifiers are used to expand nouns in both the subject and complement functions.

The **handsome** boy sang.	(adjective)
The **English** boy sang.	(attributive noun)
We watched the **dancing** children sing.	(verbal)
The **kind** man gave the **happy** boy a **lovely** gift.	(adjectives)
The **backward** boy had to repeat the class.	(adverb)
Her husband came home early.	(function word, a personal pronoun)
The **serious young** boy wore a **bright blue** coat.	(adjectives)
It is **Mary's** coat.	(possessive noun)

This coat is torn.	(function word, a determiner)
Her trip **abroad** lasted months.	(adverb)
He killed the **struggling** animal.	(verbal)

Sometimes another noun is used to modify a noun, as in the second example, "The English boy sang." When a noun occurs in this function it is called an *attributive noun*.

In the third and last examples, the single-word modifier used to expand the noun is a *verbal*. A verbal has the same characteristics as a verb—for example, it can be used in the three basic verb forms—but it functions as a noun, adjective, or adverb.

Function words known as *intensifiers*, such as "very," "more," "particularly," "exceptionally," "quite," "too," and "rather," may be used to expand noun clusters still further. For example, "The particularly handsome young English boy sang."

The usual modifiers of verbs are adverbs, but adjectives, nouns, verbs, and function words can be used as well. The placement of verb modifiers varies.

The engine stopped **suddenly**.	(adverb)
The boy marched **briskly**.	(adverb)
Hurriedly she packed her case and left the house.	(adverb)
Joe works **harder** than his brother.	(adverb)
They went **home**.	(noun)
The soldiers marched **singing**.	(verbal)
John went **out**.	(function word, a preposition)
He went every **Sunday** to church.	(noun)
The little boy went **crying** to his mother.	(verbal)
The athlete ran **fast**.	(adjective)

The predicate adjective may also be modified by a variety of language forms. The most usual modifier is an intensifier, but nouns, verbs, and adverbs may be used as well.

This rule is **quite** ridiculous.	(function word, an intensifier)
The man was **obviously** annoyed.	(adverb)
John became **very** quiet.	(function word, an intensifier)
The restless audience was anxious **to leave**.	(verbal)
John was happy **Monday**.	(noun)

Remember that the most important words in any sentence are nouns and verbs. Modifiers are important because they add meaning, color, and precision to writing, but too many can conceal the main purpose of the sentence and confuse the reader. Care must also be taken with the choice of modifiers. Over-used modifiers, such as "nice," "good," "fine," "old," "mean," "poor," "very," "big," "huge," should be avoided and those that are imaginative and give variety to writing should be chosen. A thesaurus provides a wonderful choice of possible modifiers.

Word-group modifiers. The job performed by a single-word modifier in one sentence may be performed more effectively in another by a group of words. Word-group modifiers form compact units which may or may not contain subjects and predicates. If a word group does not contain both a subject and a predicate, it is called a *phrase;* if it does, it is called a *clause.* The principal word-group modifiers are (1) prepositional phrases, (2) verbal phrases, (3) subordinate clauses, and (4) appositives.

Prepositional phrases. The most common type of word-group modifier is the prepositional phrase. It is introduced by a function word such as "above," "about," "across," "after," "against," "among," "at," "beneath," "beside," "beyond," "by," "down," "from," "in," "into," "of," "off," "on," "out," "over," "through," "to," "toward," "under," "up," and "with." These words are called *prepositions* because of their function of signaling the prepositional phrase. The following sentences are examples of modification through the use of prepositional phrases. The words modified are shown in parentheses. Prepositional phrases may be used to modify nouns, verbs, and predicate adjectives.

noun modification:
>The (view) **across the valley** was too beautiful to describe.
>The (lady) **in the back of the car** glared at the crowd.
>I took my husband to see the (house) **on the hill.**

verb modification:
>My brother (lives) **in a cottage by the sea.**
>The tennis champion (boasted) **about winning.**
>The roses (came) **into bloom early.**

predicate adjective modification:
>Joan looked (pretty) **in her new dress.**
>Peter is (first) **in his class.**
>The angry man appeared (unhappy) **about the outcome.**

Verbal phrases. Verbal phrases used as modifiers may be either participial or infinitive phrases. A *participial phrase* is made up of a participle with its modifiers and determiners. The participle may be either the present participle (usually with an *-ing* ending), or the past participle (usually with an *-ed* or *-en* ending). Participial phrases usually modify a noun or a noun substitute. In the sentence, "I stood on the balcony enjoying the magnificent view," the pronoun "I" is modified by the word-group "enjoying the magnificent view." Other examples:

>The (man), **seething with anger,** was the boy's father.
>This is my (picture), **taken on the day of my wedding.**
>The (candidate), **exhausted by the rigorous schedule,**
>   climbed into bed.

An *infinitive phrase* is made up of an infinitive with its modifiers and determiners. An infinitive is the verb form usually introduced by "to." Infinitive phrases may function as adjectives or as adverbs. The following infinitive phrases are functioning as adjectives.

(Judy) is a beautiful dancer **to watch**.

There were plenty of (apples) on the tree **to sell**.

A tidy husband is an unusual (man) **to have in the home**.

Richard Nixon is the (candidate) **to elect**.

The following infinitive phrases are functioning as adverbs.

The children (left) early **to go to the game**.

Joan often (comes) **to smell our roses**.

My parents (are coming) next month **to visit me**.

The audience (waited) **to see the play**.

Subordinate clauses. Subordinate clauses differ from phrases in that they contain both subject and predicate. Two kinds of subordinate clauses function as modifiers: adjectival clauses and adverbial clauses. *Adjectival clauses* modify nouns or noun substitutes. They are introduced by words such as "who," "whose," "whom," "which," "that," "when," "where," and "why." These words, together with those used to introduce adverbial clauses, are function words called *subordinators*. The following sentences contain examples of adjectival clauses.

The (marigold), **which Senator Dirksen maintains should be the national flower**, has the most beautiful color.

Here are the (flowers) **that you asked me to pick**.

We went to the (restaurant) **that we went to before we were married**.

Adverbial clauses usually modify verbs and the linking verbs in the N-LV-A sentence pattern, but they can also be used to modify predicate adjectives, adverbs, and verb forms (participles or infinitives) themselves functioning as modifiers. The subordinators "when," "where," "why," "how," "as," "though," "before," "after," "until," "unless," "because," "since," "if," "while," and "although" introduce adverbial clauses.

verb modification:

They (will come) home early **if they can catch a train**.

He agreed (to come) home early **although he did not want to.**
The children (cried) **when they got home.**
He (wondered) **why they were leaving.**

predicate adjective modification:
Joan became (sick) **when she saw how high we were.**
This method is (easier) **than we had hoped for.**
He was (sorry) **that he could not come to tea.**

adverb modification:
This fish struggled (harder) **than the other one did** when it was pulled out of the water.
The skier went so (fast) down the slope **that he nearly fell.**
The comedian talked (quickly) **as the program neared the end.**

verbal modification:
We enjoy (caroling) **when it is Christmas time.**
He will go (to work) **when the bell rings.**

Appositives. Appositives may also be used to expand sentences. They are parallel structures which give additional information about the nouns they follow. They may be single words (usually nouns, although adjectives may also be used), phrases, or clauses.

(John Brown), **our new neighbor,** has a blue car.	(noun phrase)
(The town), **dirty and unattractive,** lay beneath us.	(adjectives)
(His sports car), **the oldest one in the neighborhood,** needs painting.	(adjectival phrase)
(The girl had one dream), **to marry a handsome and wealthy man.**	(infinitive phrase)

The four types of word-group modifiers must be placed near the words they modify. If they are misplaced, they may change rather than expand the meaning of the sentence. An ill-placed modifier is called a *misplaced* or *dangling* modifier. Notice how misplaced modifiers make the following sentences unclear.

> The dress is owned by that girl with the red designs.
> He pushed the cart along the street full of garbage.

Sometimes it is best to rewrite such a sentence completely, but usually a shift in the position of the modifier is adequate.

> That girl owns the dress with the red designs.
> He pushed the cart full of garbage along the street.

Another common error is to modify a word that is not there. For example,

> Sailing down the river, it was possible to see the stars.

Such a sentence should be revised by including the missing word:

> Sailing down the river, I could see the stars.

Or it may be rewritten entirely:

> As I sailed down the river, I could see the stars.

Modifying Kernel Sentence Patterns

Just as individual words within the kernel sentences may be expanded through modification, the kernel sentence patterns themselves may be expanded. Sentence patterns are expanded mainly in two ways—through subordination, and through coordination. A third, less significant, way is through the addition of an unrelated structure called an absolute structure.

Subordination. Sentences may be expanded through the introduction of a subordinate clause. For example, the sentence, "We shall have dinner on the patio," is expanded as a whole by the introduction of the subordinate clause "when the evenings are warmer":

> When the evenings are warmer, we shall have dinner on the patio.

A kernel sentence expanded by subordination is called a *complex sentence*. The two subordinating word-group modifiers, the adjectival clause and the adverbial clause, may be used to modify sentences. A third subordinating word group, the *noun clause*, may also be used for this purpose. The noun clause substitutes for a noun in any of its functions. The use of the noun clause is shown in the following examples.

as a subject:
> **What she will do** is still a mystery.
> **How she got there** is unimportant.

as a direct object:
> The author hoped **that his book would sell**.
> He suddenly realized **what was wrong**.

as a linking-verb complement:
> The fact is **that we forgot to tell her**.
> My problem is **how I can afford it**.

as the object of a preposition:
> There was some doubt as to **where we should go**.
> We must go by **whichever road is best**.

as the object of a verbal:
> Realizing **what would happen**, he slowly crept forward.
> He said he would do anything to discover **what was in the chest**.

Coordination. Kernel sentences may also be expanded by coordination, the joining of two or more similar grammatical structures. Any part of a basic sentence pattern may be coordinated, or the whole sentence may be joined to another sentence. When the coordination appears in the subject form it is called subject noun coordination or a "compound subject." When it appears in the predicate it is called predicate coordination or a "compound predicate"; when the verb is coordinated it is called a "compound verb," and so on. A kernel sentence pattern expanded by coordination is thus called a *compound sentence*.

> John came home.   (kernel sentence)

John and **Mary** came home.	(simple subject noun coordination or compound subject)
The men **smoked** their pipes and **drank** their beer.	(predicate coordination or compound predicate)
Ethel carried a **raincoat** and an **umbrella**.	(complement coordination or compound direct object)
He went to the **supermarket** and to the **drugstore**.	(complement coordination or compound indirect object)
Bright red and **yellow** pansies filled the vase.	(modifier coordination or compound modifier)
The stars were twinkling in the sky and the moon was shining brightly as we left the party.	(sentence coordination or compound sentence)

Absolute structures. A third way in which kernel sentences may be expanded is through the introduction of absolute structures. An absolute structure is an independent structure which expands the meaning of a sentence but is not necessary to its structure or its sense. That is, it does not have a specific function within the sentence. For example,

> **To tell the truth,** I don't like the hat you are wearing.

Absolute structures are commonly made up of nouns modified by *-ing* or *-ed* participles, which are sometimes accompanied by auxiliaries.

> **Weather permitting,** we will go sailing tomorrow.
> **His gardening finished,** John lay out in the sun.

Sometimes prepositional and verbal phrases are used as absolute structures.

> **To say the least,** his act was scandalous.
> **Off the record,** I would say that he is a crook.

Punctuation: The Mechanics of Sentence Structure

When we speak, we use three devices to make our expression meaningful and clear: (1) pitch, the rise and fall of our voices; (2) stress or accent; and (3) juncture, the pauses we make between words and phrases. For example, our voices rise at the ends of questions. ("Are you going out?" "You are going out?") When we are surprised, our voices become more highly pitched. ("Really?" "My goodness!") We stress words when we want to emphasize them. ("That was an *excellent* meal.") We pause between words and phrases when we want to emphasize them or to indicate a change in thought. ("John, the boy who lives next door, is always late for school. . . . I ran home to get supper, but my husband had already eaten his. . . . I was so tired, I went straight to bed.") The rhythm and clarity we achieve in speech must be conveyed in our writing. This is achieved, as nearly as possible, by the use of punctuation.

The Functions of Punctuation

The essential functions of punctuation are (1) to separate structurally unrelated units of language, and (2) to separate words within sentences.

To Separate Unrelated Units of Language

Punctuation is used to mark off the basic structural units of language, sentences. A sentence may be terminated by several different marks depending upon its content, but each mark indicates a complete structural separation from the sentences or words that precede and follow it. Statements, commands, and indirect questions are terminated by periods (.). Direct questions are terminated by question marks (?). Exclamations are terminated by exclamation points (!).

The train leaves at noon.	(statement)
Don't miss the train.	(command)
He asked whether the train had left.	(indirect question)

> Has the train left?   (question)
> The train has left!   (exclamation)

To Separate Words Within Sentences

Punctuation is used within sentences to mark off supplementary structures, single words or word groups, that might otherwise be confused with the basic subject-predicate structure of the sentence. It prevents misinterpretation.

> Tom thought Harry was cowardly.
> Tom, thought Harry, was cowardly.

Several marks may be used for this purpose: comma, semicolon, colon, dash, and parentheses. The comma, which indicates the smallest degree of separation, is usually sufficient to clarify the relationships among the words of most sentences; however, colons, dashes, and parentheses are used to indicate greater degrees of separation. The use of the semicolon is more restricted: it separates word groups in a series when the word groups themselves contain commas, and it can take the place of a coordinator in a compound sentence.

For example, *subordinate clauses* are usually set off with commas, although dashes and parentheses are sometimes used.

> Although he had not seen me for many years, he remembered me.
> The bride, after she had cut the cake with her husband, threw her bouquet to her bridesmaids.

Appositives are usually set off with commas, although dashes and parentheses are occasionally used.

> The bride, formerly Miss Brown, looked beautiful.
> Her outfit, a lace dress and veil that had been worn by her mother, fitted extremely well.

Absolute structures are set off with commas.

> The wedding over, the guests departed.

A *series of modifiers* attached to the same word or word group is separated by commas.

> Her bright blue, short, velvet dress was unusual.
> The application form should be filled out completely, accurately, legibly.

Quotations contained within sentences are usually set off by commas.

> She said, "I must see you."
> "I need a new dress," she said, "and I want you to buy me one."

However, a long quotation at the end of a sentence is usually introduced by a colon.

> The minister opened his sermon with the following words:
> "We are often troubled by. . . ."

In *coordinated sentences,* words or word groups in a series are usually separated by commas.

> Jane, Mary, and Anne were her bridesmaids.
> We gave her the scissors, the material, the thread, and the buttons, and asked her to make the dress.
> The children hopped, skipped, and jumped down the street.

However, semicolons may be used when the word groups themselves contain commas.

> The three girls who won prizes for home economics are Joan, the pretty blonde girl; Ethel, the girl who sews so well; and Lynn, the girl sitting over there.

A colon may be used to introduce a list or items in a series.

> Here are some solutions to the problem: we must first of all organize ourselves; then we must obtain some money; and then we must find the best things to buy.

In *compound sentences,* when the two sentences patterns are joined by a coordinator, a comma is used to separate them.

> He crept quietly into the room, but we all saw him.

When a coordinator is not used, a stronger separation is needed. A semicolon is usual, although colons and dashes are sometimes used.

> The plane taxied to a standstill; three men climbed out.
> He is seriously ill: the doctor suspects pneumonia.
> He crept quietly into the room—we all saw him.

Punctuation is used to clarify the structure of language, and by clarifying structure, it clarifies meaning.

The Punctuation Marks

The *period* (.) indicates the end of a statement, command, or an indirect question.

The *exclamation point* (!) indicates the end of a sentence or sentence fragment that expresses surprise or strong emotion.

The *question mark* (?) indicates the end of a question.

The *comma* (,) is used within sentences to set off supplementary structures, single words or word groups, that might otherwise confuse the meaning of the basic sentence. It represents the least separation, or smallest interruption in structural pattern, of any of the punctuation marks used for this purpose. In addition to marking off modifying structures, quotations, and items in series, as shown in the examples above, the comma has various special uses. For example, it is used between the day or month and the year in dates:

> I hope to go to Europe in March, 1969.
> This magazine is dated February 1, 1958.

It is used between the parts of an address used in a sentence.

> He lives at Apartment 2, Concord House, Mission Road, Boston, Massachusetts.

It is also used at the end of salutations and complimentary closings in letters.

The *semicolon* (;) is used, as shown in the above examples, to separate the two sentence patterns in a compound sentence when a coordinator is not used. It indicates strong separation, and may be used only to separate complete sentence patterns in compound sentences. The exception is its special use—separating word groups in a series when the word groups themselves contain commas.

The *colon* (:) indicates that the words to follow it contain an illustration or amplification of the words preceding it. It is therefore used to introduce lists and series of words or phrases, and to introduce long formal quotations, as in the examples above. It is also used to separate the two sentence patterns in a compound sentence when a coordinator is not used and when the second sentence explains, amplifies, or illustrates the first. The colon also has several special uses. For example, it is used after the formal salutation of a letter ("Dear Sir:"), between the hours and minutes in expressing the time of day ("9:06 A.M."), and in Biblical references ("Genesis 2:8-9"). It is also used between the title and subtitle of a book, and in footnote references to separate the city of publication from the publisher's name.

> Jane Ervin, *A Short Guide to the New Grammar: The Contemporary Approach to the Teaching of English* (Los Angeles: Tinnon-Brown, Inc., 1968).

The *dash* (–) is used between parts of a sentence in the same way that a comma is used. However, it signals a more abrupt break in structure and should be used sparingly because it can interrupt continuity of meaning. It may also be used to separate the two sentence patterns in a compound sentence when a coordinator is not used.

Parentheses ( ), like the comma and the dash, are used to set apart supplementary words that are not part of the basic sentence pattern. Parentheses, however, usually indicate that the supplementary information is so loosely related to the main thought of the sentence that it could possibly be contained in a separate sentence. For example, "This house (no longer for sale) has high taxes." Parentheses may also be used to set apart an entire sentence that is not closely related in thought or logical continuity to the sentences preceding and following it.

The *apostrophe* (') has several uses. It is used in showing possession: "the girl's hat" (singular), "the girl's hats" (double), "Joan and Mary's hats" (double). It marks the omission of letters in the contraction of words and of figures in numbers: "it's here" for "it is here"; "he hasn't left" for "he has not left"; " '68" for "1968." It is used in forming the plurals of letters and numbers: "1960's"; "p's and q's." Two apostrophes, or single quotes, are used to set off words whose origins or meanings are being discussed:

> Blessé is French for 'wounded'—not 'blessed' as one might think.
> The development of 'shelter' is interesting.

Single quotes are also used to set off secondary quotations, or quotations that appear in material that is itself set off by quotation marks.

Quotation marks (") are used to enclose statements that are being repeated exactly as they were spoken or as they were written in some other place.

> He said, "I must leave immediately."

A sign on the door read "Please knock."
The article began: "During the last war...."

In books, long passages of quoted material may be printed in smaller type than the rest of the text and placed in separate paragraphs; when this is done, quotation marks are not necessary. Quotation marks are also used to call attention to particular or unusual words, or words that are being used out of their usual structural contexts.

You should always use "and" and "but" in these sentences.
In the sentence, "The girl came into the room," the word "girl" is the headword of the noun phrase.
We shall discuss the concepts "right" and "wrong."

Quotation marks are also used to set off the titles of articles, stories, poems, songs, and other short compositions.

Italic type is used to set off words or word groups to which special reference is being made. For example, it is being used to set off the topic of this paragraph. It is also used as a visual form of the stress and accent we use in speaking to emphasize words. Special uses of italic type are to set off foreign words and phrases, and to indicate the titles of books, magazines, plays, and longer musical compositions.

Chapter Two
The Functions of Words

The Word Classes

In the first chapter, we saw that our basic unit of communication is the sentence. We discovered that the sentence is always made up of a subject followed by a predicate (which may or may not contain a complement), and that if we want to communicate effectively, we must arrange our words in this order. Words do have meanings in themselves—their "lexical" or "dictionary" meanings—but only when they are arranged in subject-predicate order do they convey a complete, coherent message. Each of the following words conveys some meaning, "day was very it hot a"; but only when the words are arranged in subject-predicate order do they *go beyond* their lexical meanings to communicate a coherent message, "It was a very hot day."

Some words convey more lexical meaning than others; these words are the most important and form the basis of our language. They are called *nouns* and *verbs*. The next in importance are the words we add to give extra meaning and power to the nouns and verbs. They are called modifiers. There are two kinds of modifiers: *adjectives* and *adverbs*. These four word classes—nouns, verbs, adjectives, and adverbs—are sometimes called *content words*, and they constitute over 90 per cent of our total language. When new words are added to our lexicon, they fall into one of these word classes.

All of our other English words are called *function words* or "structure words." They have very little lexical meaning in themselves, but they serve an indispensable function in sentences by clarifying the relationships among the content words. Function words can be grouped into several subclasses. They are *auxiliaries, determiners, intensifiers, connectives,* (prepositions, coordinators, and subordinators), and *pronouns* (personal, indefinite, intensifying, and relative).

The five word classes or word forms:
1. nouns
2. verbs
3. adjectives ⎱
4. adverbs   ⎰ modifiers
5. function words

The Primary Functions Within Sentences

Because word order is the most important aspect of our language, we study words in terms of their relationships to other words and in terms of their positions within sentences—that is, we study words by examining their functions within sentences.

The most important, or primary, functions within a sentence are the subject, the predicate, the complement, and the modifier. Secondary functions include the object of a preposition, the appositive, and the absolute construction. No single word form preempts any one function except the verb, which always forms part of the predicate. For example, although a noun most frequently occurs in the subject function, adjectives, adverbs, verbals, and even determiners may also function there. The wide variety of forms that may perform in each primary function of the sentence is shown in the following examples.

The Subject Function

The noun occurs most often in the subject function of sentences.

> The **postman** delivered the letter.
> The **gypsies** moved their camp during the night.
> A **trapper** gave these snowshoes to the scout.

However, verbals also occur in this function.

the participle or participial phrase (when the present or -*ing* form is used in the noun function it is called a *gerund*):
>   **Swimming** is excellent exercise.
>   **Swimming twenty-five meters every day** should keep you in shape.

the infinitive or infinitive phrase:
>   **To graduate from college** is a fine goal.
>   **To ski successfully** takes much practice.
>   **To sink and swim** is a paradox.

Modifiers occur in the subject function.
>   the adjective:
>>   The **meek** are not necessarily weak.
>>   The **poor** are often exploited.

>   the adverb:
>>   **Yesterday** is always too late, and **tomorrow** is too soon.
>>   **Now** is the time to do your work.

Function words may also be used in the subject function.
>   the determiner:
>>   **Thirteen** is an unlucky number.
>>   **This** is the kidnapper.
>>   **All** of us were invited but **none** of us went.

>   the personal pronoun:
>>   **She** washed the dishes after the party.
>>   **I** like to go to the circus.
>>   **They** might have been good friends.

>   the indefinite pronoun:
>>   **Everybody** had a good time at Cynthia's party.
>>   **Nobody** liked the escargots.
>>   **Anybody** can drive a car, even Auntie Myrtle!

the connective (relative pronoun):

> There is the man **who** painted our house.
> We sailed on the boat **that** goes around the Cape of Good Hope.
> John chose this champagne, **which** was imported from France.

In addition to participial and infinitive phrases, other modifying word groups may be used.

the prepositional phrase:

> **Across the beach** is a long walk.
> **Over the plate between the knees and shoulders** is a strike.

the subordinate noun clause:

> **What this child needs** is some old-fashioned discipline.
> **That your homework fell in the mud** is no excuse.
> **Where they will go on their honeymoon** is a secret.

The Predicate Verb Function

The verb, of course, occurs most often in the predicate verb function.

> Willie Mays **hit** the ball out of the park.
> They **flew** to San Francisco.
> The lost child **cried** all the way to the police station.

However, words from other classes may be used in this function.

the noun:

> The rancher **branded** his animals.
> He **pruned** his rose bushes.
> The parrot **mimicked** the dog's bark.

the adjective:

>She **reddened** with embarrassment at his remark.
>She **brightened** my day.
>We **quieted** the crying child.

the adverb:

>He **quickened** his pace near the park.
>We **furthered** the civil rights cause.
>He **slowed** for the curve in the road.

function words:

>The fighter **K.O.'d** his opponent.
>**Zot! Zowey! Swack! Pow!**
>He **humbugged** the idea.

The Complement Function

Nouns or noun phrases most commonly appear in the complement function.

>We unearthed six old **skulls** in the Indian burial grounds.
>Miss Jones is **my English teacher**.
>The fishermen of the North Atlantic catch **cod and mackerel**.

Adjectives and adverbs may also function as complements.
the adjective:

>These pears look **green and hard**.
>The wind seems **icy and cold** today.
>The sky is **blue**.

the adverb:

>The meeting is **tomorrow**.
>The meeting will be **here**.

Function words sometimes occur in the complement function.
   the personal pronoun:

> A gold watch was given **him** on his retirement.
> The interviewer asked **her** a question.

   the indefinite pronoun:

> Some people want **everything**.
> He was **nobody** until he was elected president.

   the determiner:

> I have **one**.
> Here are **several** from which you may select **three**.

   the connective:

> John is the kind of man **whom** you should hire.
> We found an old copper plate **where** the fireplace had stood.

Other modifiers and modifying word groups may function as complements.
   the participle or participial phrase:

> Bill likes **watching television**.
> Susan enjoys **bowling**.
> They looked **excited**.
> Roger and Ann appeared **delighted with the gift**.
> The children seem **excited at the prospect of going to Disneyland**.

   the infinitive or infinitive phrase:

> Mark wanted **to buy** the house immediately.
> I like **to sleep late on Saturday**.

I came **to see** if you wanted me.

the subordinate noun clause:

Margie realizes **what she must do to get an "A."**
My father explained **how he caught the sea turtle.**

The Noun-Modifying Function
The usual modifiers of nouns are adjectives.

The **soft** thud of hoofs came from the **hidden** trail.
The **angry** group stood before the **old** courthouse.
The **long** train of covered wagons crept across the **hot dusty** plain.

However, nouns may be used to modify other nouns.
the possessive noun:

That is my **mother's** new dress.
We passed by the little brown **monkey's** cage.

the attributive noun, or modifying noun:

Bill is the **American** representative at the conference.
The **court** stenographer recorded the testimony.
The **car** radio was playing loudly.

Function words may be used to modify nouns.
the personal pronoun:

Her engagement ring is very unusual.
Is this **your** coat and purse?
My mother is pleased with **her** new coat.

the connective (relative pronoun):

This is the man **whose** house you admire.

The boy **who** is tallest will lead the parade.
She told her mother **which** dress she wanted.

the determiner:

This glass is broken.
We looked over **several** cars before buying **this** one.

Other single-word modifiers and modifying word groups may be used to modify nouns.
the adverb:

The **backward** child found the new reader difficult.
The house's position **here** will protect you from the winds.

the participle or participial phrase:

The **closing** scene of the play is disasterous.
A **traveling** salesman has a difficult life.
The fellow **sailing in the race** is my boyfriend.
Spoken language was the most important form of
    communication for thousands of years.
The **developed** film was used as evidence in the case.
The foresters gathered up the **broken** branches.

the infinitive or infinitive phrase:

The only way **to fly** is by jet.
John has an appointment with the doctor **to see**
    if his arm is broken.
The movement **to gain more vacation time** is well underway.

the prepositional phrase:

The hedge **around the garden** has been cut.

The piece **of clear glass** shone like new silver.
They found the key **to the door** underneath the loose board.

the subordinate adjectival clause:

The idea **that you developed** is being discussed by the committee.
The boy **whom you see on the tightwire** is my brother.
The clouds, **which hung halfway down the mountain sides**, hid the top of the range completely.

The Verb-Modifying Function
The adverb is the most usual modifier of verbs.

The children laughed **loudly** and **merrily**.
I will help you **soon**.
We could call **aloud**.

However, other types of words and word groups may function as verb modifiers.
the noun:

I go **home** for lunch.
The ship will arrive **Friday**.
The accident happened last **night**.

the adjective:

Jane always presses **hard** when she writes.
He bid too **low** to get the auctioned furniture.
I hid too **long** in the poison ivy.

the function word (preposition):

I saw the village lights **below**.
We have never played this game **before**.
The dog jumped **up**.

the infinitive or infinitive phrase:

> A competitive skier needs **to ski five hours a day to keep in shape.**
> The men went to the orchard **to pick the ripe fruit.**
> Susan was sent **to arrange the window display.**

the participle or participial phrase (present or *-ing* form):

> The horse came **galloping** toward us.
> Aunt Maude likes **watching** the neighbors from her parlor window.
> The book went **flying** toward the window.

the prepositional phrase:

> This letter from my father was delivered **by special messenger before noon.**
> The boys jumped **into the icy water.**
> We were walking **on a carpet of soft grass.**

the subordinate adverbial clause:

> My father read the paper **while mother cooked breakfast.**
> We'll wait for you **where the road turns west.**
> I left **when it got dark.**

The Functions of Content Words

Having observed how the primary functions of the sentence can be performed by a variety of word classes, let us now observe the specific functions performed by each content word class.

Functions Performed by Nouns

Nouns function in sentences mainly as subjects, complements, and objects of prepositions, but they may perform a variety of other functions. The position of a noun in a sentence determines its function. Nouns are always the headwords of noun phrases:

the noun provides the key to the meaning of the noun phrase.

> nouns as the subjects of sentences:
>
>> The **airplane** was flying low.
>> The **tumbleweed** scatters its seeds in the wind.
>> Salty sea **air** spreads through the streets like a dense fog.
>
> nouns as the subjects of subordinate clauses:
>
>> The log house stands where the **creek** joins the river.
>> That house was built before the first white **man** crossed the Sierra Nevada.
>> After **Oregon** was acquired by the United States, it was soon made a territory.
>
> nouns as the subjects of infinitives:
>
>> They chopped the **wood** to put on the fire.
>> John told **Mary** to budget more carefully.
>
> nouns as the direct objects of verbs:
>
>> Jack hit the **ball** over the fence.
>> She broke her **leg** when she jumped from the chair lift.
>> The chairman introduced the **speaker.**
>
> nouns as the direct objects of verbals:
>
>> Unleashing the **dogs** was the last step in the search for the lost man.
>> Mother told me to practice my **music** before father got home.
>
> nouns as indirect objects:
>
>> Mary gave her **husband** a new typewriter.

The nurse passed the **doctor** the sterilized instruments.
Please pass **Fred** the plate of cookies.

nouns as objective complements:

Mr. Oaks made his son a **partner** in the business.
The President considered him the best **man** for the job.

nouns as linking-verb complements:

The beauty queen is the **image** of the typical American girl.
The Smiths were the **owners** of the stolen get-away car.
Sam became **president** of the company at thirty-three.

nouns as the objects of prepositions:

The silk curtains at the front **window** were soiled and torn.
The trees in our front **yard** were planted by my **grandfather**.
The city lay between the two **lakes**.

nouns as appositives:

He depended upon you, his best **friend**, to carry on for him.
Our neighbor, **Mr. Williams**, took us to the airport.
That star is Vega, the brightest **star** in the summer sky.

nouns as headwords in absolute constructions:

Her **eyes** misty, Mary watched her sister marry Bob.
Their **game** over, the players were rewarded with hot showers and steak dinners.

nouns as attributive nouns:

The **student** newspaper published the true facts of the story.

Spencer Jones is the **county** clerk.
The **weather** forecast was not in the paper today.

nouns as possessive modifiers:

That is **Sara's** mother buying that sweater.
The new television program will advertise **men's** shaving lotion.
The **children's** bedtime is seven o'clock.

nouns as adverbs:

She plans to sail the **President Line.**
I will be home **Monday** afternoon.

Functions Performed by Verbs

Verbs are the most important words in the English language because they provide the basic structure around which sentence patterns are developed and therefore indicate the chief substance of our communications. Verbs are complex words which cannot be described easily, and in fact grammarians today seem unable to come up with a truly foolproof analysis of their forms and functions. All accept the obvious fact that there are "regular" and "irregular" verbs, but none seem able to agree on the regularities and irregularities.

It appears, however, that it is possible to divide verbs into four-part regular verbs and five-part, four-part, and three-part irregular verbs. The four basic forms of the regular verbs are (1) the simple or infinitive, (2) the past, (3) the present participle, and (4) the third person singular in the present tense.

infinitive	**past**	**present participle**	**third person singular in the present tense**
(to) walk	walked	walking	walks
(to) stay	stayed	staying	stays
(to) jump	jumped	jumping	jumps
(to) move	moved	moving	moves

By studying the above examples, it is easy to see that the change in form occurs through changes in the inflectional endings of the verb. The past is formed by adding the morpheme *-ed,* the present participle by adding the morpheme *-ing,* and the third person singular in the present tense by adding the morpheme *-s.* (The inflectional forms of irregular verbs are given in detail in the following chapter.)

Although verbs can be inflected in five, four, or three ways depending on the kinds of regular or irregular verbs they are, basically they can only indicate two *tenses* or two basic times: the present and the past. For example,

present	past
I walk	I walked
they jump	they jumped

Verbs can indicate many other times but only through combination with auxiliaries, function words such as "have," "had," "will," "can," "do," and "might," which were described earlier on page 26. It is the many different combinations that can be made with auxiliaries that enables verbs to function in so many varied and subtle ways. In fact, the English verb, when functioning with auxiliaries, is probably one of the most flexible to be found in any language.

Functions of the Four Basic Forms of Regular Verbs

The infinitive form. The infinitive form, sometimes called the simple or plain form, is used to express the present tense (except in the third person singular.

The musicians **play** extremely well.

Teachers usually **rest** during the summer vacation.

You **come** to me.

When the infinitive form is combined with auxiliaries such as "can," "could," "do," "does," "did," "may," "might," "must," "shall," "should," "will," and "would," it can express a variety of subtle meanings and tenses. For example,

    I **will play** with my sister.   (meaning sometime later, in the future)
    I **might play** with my sister.   (meaning it is possible)
    I **could play** with my sister.   (meaning it is possible)
    I **should play** with my sister.   (meaning I ought to)
    I **must play** with my sister.   (meaning I ought to)

The infinitive form of three-part irregular verbs serves two additional functions: it is used as the past form to indicate past tense, and as the past participle when combined with an auxiliary or combination of auxiliaries. For example,

    I **hit** the boy.   (present)
    I **hit** the boy.   (past)
    The tree has **shed** its leaves.   (past participle)

The infinitive form of the four-part irregular verbs "come" and "run" also functions as the past participle when combined with an auxiliary or combination of auxiliaries. For example,

    He has **run** in the Olympic Games before.   (past participle)
    The letter should have **come** last week.   (past participle)

The past form. The past form functions to tell of something that has occurred or existed before. For example,

    I **played** tennis.
    The boys **moved** their toys to the den.

The past form is also used with certain auxiliaries in the past participle function. When it is combined with the auxiliaries "has" or "have" it is used to tell of something that occurred at some indefinite time in the past or that began in the past and continues into the present. For example,

> He **has played** this game before.   (occurred in the past)
> We **have played** this game for ten
>   years.   (occurred in the past, continues into present)

When the past form is combined with the auxiliary "had," it functions to tell of something that happened in the past before something else happened. For example,

> earlier: later:
> We **had played**   before the girls arrived.

The present participle form. The present participle form functions with the auxiliaries "am," "is," "are," "was," "were," "keep," "keeps," and "kept," and with combinations of certain auxiliaries such as "has" and "had" and "be" and "been." For example,

> I am **keeping** my mind open.
> The children are **looking** for their toys.
> The boys kept **teasing** the girls.
> John has been **joking** all day.
> They should have been **studying**.
> I shall be **watching** you carefully.

The third person singular form. This form is used solely to indicate the third person singular in the present tense. It is formed by adding the morpheme -*s* to the infinitive. For example,

> regular verb (walk): he **walks**
> five-part irregular verb (begin): he **begins**
> four-part irregular verb (feed): he **feeds**
> three-part irregular verb (quit): he **quits**

The Flexibility of Verbs

The wide variety of tenses and of subtle meanings that can be conveyed by verbs, used alone or combined with auxiliaries, is shown in the following examples.

tense	example	function
present	I walk	Tells of something that exists or is happening at the moment: "I **walk** when the evenings are light."
past	I walked	Tells of something that existed or happened in the past: "I **walked** home quickly."
present-past (present-perfect)	I have walked	Tells of something that occurred at some definite time in the past or that began in the past and continues into the present: "I have walked along here before" (occurred in the past); "I have walked along here for six years" (and still do).
past-past (past-perfect)	I had walked	Tells of something that occurred in the past before something else occurred: "I had walked down the path before I noticed that the gate was closed."
future	I will walk	Tells of something that has not yet occurred: "I will walk down the path after you open the gate."

tense	example	function
future-past	I will have walked	Tells of something completed in the future before something else occurs: "When I reach home I will have walked three miles."

In addition to placing actions or events in time, verbs can be used to convey other information about them. For example, verbs can be used to indicate that an action or event is, was, or will be "on-going," that is, continuing over a period of time.

I am walking.	(present)
I have been walking.	(present-past)
I had been walking.	(past-past)
I will be walking.	(future)

Verbs can be used to give special emphasis. For example,

I do walk.	(present)
I did walk.	(past)

Verbs can also be used to express obligation, intention, possibility, hope, or prayer (this function is called "subjunctive" in traditional grammar). For example,

> I should walk.
> I might walk.
> I ought to walk.

Most verbs function either as transitive or intransitive verbs according to their uses in particular sentences.

The losing team held a hasty meeting.	(transitive)
A hasty meeting was held.	(intransitive)

In the transitive form, the verb passes the action it expresses over to an object. In the N-V-N and N-V-N-N patterns, the verb is always transitive because there is always a direct object. In the N-V pattern, the verb is intransitive because there is no object. All linking verbs function as intransitive verbs.

    N   V   N
Joan played tennis.   (transitive)

    N   V   N   N
Joan gave her brother a cup of tea.   (transitive)

   N V
He lost.   (intransitive)

    N   LV   N
Patricia will be my partner.   (intransitive)

    N   LV   A
The cake tasted good.   (intransitive)

Verbs may function either in the active or passive voice. When functioning in the active voice, the verb takes a direct object. When functioning in the passive voice, the verb appears in the past participle form with the verb "to be"; it is usually followed by a prepositional phrase beginning with "by"; and its direct object becomes the subject. A verb changes from the active voice to the passive voice by means of transformation.

	subject	verb	direct object
active:	Joan	baked	a cake.
	subject	verb	"by" prepositional phrase
passive:	The cake	was baked	by Joan.

Verb Functions Apart from Predication
The main function of verbs is predication but they can also perform in other functions. Verbs performing in functions other than predication are *verbals: infinitives, participles,* and *gerunds* (the *-ing* participle used in the noun function). The following examples show the ways in which verbals can be used.

infinitives as the subjects of sentences:

> **To write** well is not easy.
> **To disagree** with the old man seems disrespectful.
> **To have said** what you thought would have been unwise.

infinitives as direct objects:

> The bank refused **to lend** her the money.
> The artist has attempted **to illustrate** the story.
> The child wanted **to cry**.

infinitives as linking-verb complements:

> My first impulse was **to reply** angrily.
> You seemed **to hear** them.
> He appears **to be** sad over his loss.

infinitives as modifiers of nouns:

> The Peace Corps is the organization **to join**.
> The person **to ask** is Mrs. Brown.

infinitives as modifiers of verbs:

> The other school came **to play** us in football.
> She went out in the rain **to buy** the birthday cake.
> I came **to see** my sister.

infinitives as modifiers of predicate adjectives:

> It is rude **to laugh** so shrilly.
> It is useless **to refuse** his generosity.
> John seemed anxious **to leave** early.

infinitives as modifiers of predicate adverbs:

> John looked back **to see** if Lucy was following.
> We decided never **to go** there again.

infinitives as non-finite structures in a subject-predicate word group (when the infinitive is preceded by a noun or noun substitute as the subject of the infinitive):

> Her guardian told her **to go** to Europe for the summer.
> The girl asked the champion **to sign** his autograph.
> Martha helped her mother **(to) get** the dinner.

infinitives functioning as non-finite structures may also function as the objects of prepositions:

> I know it's right for you **to go** to university.
> The teacher hurried across the room **to see** what the noise was about.

infinitives as appositives:

> The teacher's assignment, **to read** *Crime and Punishment*, was greeted with dismay.
> Mrs. Jones' wish, **to buy** a house, was finally realized last summer.
> Winston's hope, **to keep** the hurt bird, was dimmed when his mother saw the creature.

infinitives as absolute structures:

> **To tell** the truth, I think he is going to be beaten.
> **To cut** a long story short, he did.

present participles as the subjects of sentences:

Shopping is very tiring.
Having lost the letter worried her.
Working faster was impossible.

present participles as direct objects:

Mike finds **working** as a box boy in the grocery store tiring.
The law forbids **smoking** inside theaters.

present participles as linking-verb complements:

My greatest pleasure is **reading** poetry.
I kept **making** the same mistake.
The barbequed steak smelled **enticing**.

present participles as objects of prepositions:

She did not approve of our **sewing** steadily.
We are thinking of **enrolling** in the swim class.

present participles as appositives:

Cinderella's wish, **marrying** the handsome prince, was to be fulfilled.
Joan has a new diet, **going** without food.

present participles as modifiers of nouns:

Shouting loudly, the man warned us of the falling ladder.
Those **screaming** children bother my husband.

present participles as modifiers of verbs:

The mourners were taken **weeping** to the cemetery.
The principal came **sweeping** into the room, demanding to see Bob.

present participles as predicate adjectives:

>A salesman's job is extremely **tiring**.
>The movie was really **amusing**.

present participles as objective complements:

>She found the long journey by train **exhausting**.
>They discovered the lost child **crying** for his mother.

past participles as modifiers of nouns:

>We decided that **fried** chicken was too fattening.
>**Frightened** by the thunder, the child buried his head in the pillow.

past participles as linking-verb complements:

>She seemed **disgusted** by his behavior.
>He looked **tired** after his difficult interview.
>The phonograph record sounded **scratched**.

Functions Performed by Adjectives

Adjectives have two main functions—they act as modifiers (usually of nouns) and as complements.

adjectives as noun modifiers:

>Five disappointed men plodded across the **muddy** field.
>**Large** rolling masses of **white** clouds were banked in the **western** sky.

adjectives as verb modifiers:

>She called **long** and **loud**.
>Sam swims very **fast**.

adjectives as linking-verb complements:

I am very **thirsty** after our long hike.
The new suit seemed **small** for me.
The tires on mine are not **good** enough for a long run.

adjectives as objective complements:

The doctors found him **healthy**.
The competitors thought the race **difficult**.
She thought the dress **pretty**.

adjectives as retained complements in the passive form:

The paper was rated **superior** by the teacher.
The food is thought **insufficient** for the party.

Functions Performed by Adverbs

Adverbs usually function as modifiers of verbs, but they also modify nouns, adjectives, and other adverbs as well as phrases and whole sentences.

adverbs as verb modifiers:

The dragonflies darted **swiftly** here and there.
The oak tree grows **slowly**.
The storm was raging **furiously**.

adverbs as modifiers of adjectives:

My skirts are **never** short.
The wind was **extremely** cold.
The **nationally** known trio will give a concert at Disneyland.

adverbs as noun modifiers:

The child drew his hand **back** from the hot stove.
My visit **tomorrow** will be a surprise.

adverbs as modifiers of adverbs:

> The car moved **slowly** forward.
> He departed **early** yesterday.

adverbs as linking-verb complements:

> The flight will be **tomorrow**.
> The mayor will be **there**.
> The mailman was already **here**.

adverbs as sentence modifiers:

> **Suddenly**, the cougar leaped on the back of the deer.
> **Despairingly**, the woman watched as the rescue team applied artificial respiration.

adverbs as verbal modifiers:

> Inching **gradually** along the ledge, the man made his way to safety.
> Hissing **furiously**, the experiment blew up the laboratory.

The Functions of Function Words

As their name implies, function words play very important parts in the structure of the sentence. Although they have little meaning on their own, they are indispensable in binding together the various content words, giving meaning and coherence to the sentence as a whole. They are also important in that they act as "signals" which identify the functions of the content words.

Notice how the following group of words is ambiguous because there are no function words to bind it together or to signal the functions of the words: "Better record results." We can interpret this to mean one of two ideas: "A better record results," or "Someone had better record the results." The inclusion of "a," "someone," "had," and "the" makes the meaning of the sentences clear.

Notice how the following sentences made up of nonsense words seem to convey a clearer meaning than the recognizable words, "Better record results." This is mainly because of the inclusion of the signaling function words, although certain characteristics of the words themselves help in their identification.

The jangor janged **the** jangent **on the** janger.
Are the jangists **going to** jang **in the** janglish?

Function words may be divided into five groups: (1) auxiliaries, (2) determiners, (3) intensifiers, (4) connectives, and (5) pronouns.

Auxiliaries

An auxiliary is a "helping" verb that is attached to a main verb, serving either as a signal for the verb or as an indication of a subtle change in its meaning, particularly in regard to time, intent, feeling, or condition. For example,

You **can** go home now.
I **may** go out this evening.
I **could have** gone out this morning.

Auxiliaries act as modifiers of the main verbs; they add to the meaning of the verb to which they are attached and have meaning only in relation to that verb. (Exceptions to this are forms of "to be," "to have," "to get," "to keep," and "to do," which can function as main verbs.)

The principal auxiliaries:

am, is, are, was, were	can, could
do, does, did	get, gets, got
going to	have, has, had
keep, keeps, kept	may, might
must	ought to
shall, should	used to
will, would	

Determiners

Determiners either directly precede the noun or precede the single-word modifiers that in turn come before the noun. They therefore serve as signals for nouns. For example, "this house," "a few old people," "that beautiful dog."

The following words act as determiners:

a, an	all	another
both	each	either
every	few	many
more	most	neither
no	none	one
other	several	some
that	the	these
this	those	what
whatever	which	whichever

Numbers are also classified as determiners, for example, "ten apples on one tree."

Determiners are sometimes used alone. This occurs when they refer to a noun or noun phrase that has already been mentioned or that is understood in the context of the sentence. In this case, the determiner is functioning as a noun substitute.

> The apples on the tree looked bad. **Many** were.
> **This** is my idea.

Intensifiers

Intensifiers are words that intensify the modifiers to which they are attached—they modify modifiers. They usually precede the modifiers, and more than one may be attached to the same word. For example,

> He was **quite** slow.
> They were **particularly** careful.
> He was fortunate **indeed**.

It was **rather too** ornate for my taste.

Words that function as intensifiers include:

exceptionally	extraordinarily	indeed
more	particularly	quite
rather	remarkably	too
unusually	very	really

Connectives

There are three kinds of connectives: (1) prepositions, (2) coordinators, and (3) subordinators. As their name implies, connectives are function words that connect word groups. They may join word groups to a basic sentence pattern, or they may join entire sentence patterns in compound sentences.

Prepositions

A preposition is followed by a noun and therefore acts as a signal for the noun. It is used to introduce a group of words called a prepositional phrase that can modify nouns, verbs, and predicate adjectives. For example, in the sentence "The beautiful yacht sailed across the bay," "across" is the preposition. It is followed by a noun, "bay," and introduces the prepositional phrase "across the bay."

The following words act as prepositions:

about	above	according to
across	after	against
along	among	around
at	because of	before
behind	below	beneath
beside	between	beyond
but for	by	concerning
down	during	except
for	from	in
in addition to	in case of	in front of

in regard to	in spite of	instead of
into	like	near
of	off	on
on account of	on behalf of	on top of
over	through	throughout
till	to	together with
toward	under	underneath
until	up	upon
with	within	without

Coordinators

Coordinators link separate words, word groups, or complete sentence patterns into one compact unit. The connection of two or more nouns is called a subject noun coordination or a "compound subject" if it appears in the subject position. If it appears in the predicate it is called complement coordination or a "compound direct object" or "compound indirect object" according to its function in the sentence. When two or more verbs are connected it is called a "compound verb." The connection of two or more sentence patterns is called a "compound sentence." For example,

John and Jean went to the theater.   (compound subject)
I gave **John and Jean** my tickets.   (compound indirect object)
The drowning man **spluttered and kicked** in desperation.   (compound verb)
I am very glad I went **but** I shall never go again.   (compound sentence)

The following words act as coordinators:

and	but	or
only	nor	so
yet	both. . . and	not (only). . .
either. . . or	neither. . . nor	but (also)

Subordinators

Subordinators are connectives that are used to join subordinate clauses (subject-predicate word groups) to a basic sentence pattern. For example,

> Here are the flowers **that** you asked me to pick.
> I went to the supermarket **after** I had been to the bank.

The following words act as subordinators:

after	although	as
before	because	how
if	since	that
though	what	when
whenever	where	wherever
whether	which	while
who	whom	whose
why	unless	until

Some grammarians classify "who," "whose," "whom," "which," and "that" as relative pronouns (see the following discussion of pronouns). Nevertheless, they recognize that when these words are used to introduce clauses they do act as connectives.

Pronouns

There is a great deal of conflict concerning the functions and characteristics of the pronoun in the New Grammar. Some grammarians limit their concept of the pronoun to what was traditionally known as the "personal" pronoun. Others include "relative" pronouns, pronouns used as intensifiers, and "indefinite" pronouns. We shall describe pronouns in terms of the latter concept because to limit our discussion to the personal pronoun would leave the function of some words in our language unaccounted for.

Personal Pronouns

The pronoun functions in a variety of different ways and in a variety of different forms, its form being closely related to its function. Personal pronouns can be inflected for person, number, gender, and case.

Person. The term "person" means the person speaking (first person), the person being spoken to (second person), and the person being spoken about (third person).

	when before the verb	when after the verb
1st person:	I	me
2nd person:	you	you
3rd person:	he, she, it	him, her, it
1st person:	we	us
2nd person:	you	you
3rd person:	they	them

Notice how the pronouns change in the subject function and the object function.

Number. The term "number" means quantity: singular or plural. Some of the singular and plural forms are shown in the list above. Below are all the singular and plural forms:

singular	plural
I, me, my, mine	we, us, our, ours
you, your, yours	you, your, yours
he, him, his	
she, her, hers	them, their, theirs
it, its	

Gender. The term "gender" means masculine, feminine, and neuter, but it occurs only in the third person singular.

masculine: he, him, his
feminine: she, her, hers
neuter: it, its

Masculine pronouns refer to male persons; they are also used when speaking in the singular form of persons in a group ("Each employee should limit his coffee break to fifteen minutes") or of unspecified persons ("Someone left his book here"). Feminine pronouns refer to female persons, and to some inanimate objects and concepts, such as ships, airplanes, and countries. Neuter pronouns refer to inanimate objects, animals whose actual genders are not known, and small creatures such as insects and reptiles.

Case. The term "case" means that the pronoun takes a particular form to indicate a particular function.

the subject forms indicate the subject function:

I, you, he, she, it; we, you, they

the possessive forms indicate the possessive function:

my, mine, your, yours, his, her, hers, its;
our, ours, their, theirs

the object forms indicate the object function:

me, you, him, her, it; us, them

Here are some examples of personal pronouns:

I would like to see **you** before **I** see **her**.
These are **mine** so those must be **yours**.
He told **me** that **they** wanted **them** to come.
Our house is larger than **yours** is.
We told **him** that **our** favorite meal is the same as **his**.

The chief functions of the personal pronoun, as these sentences show, are as noun substitutes when it is awkward or cumbersome to repeat the noun, and as noun modifiers indicating possession. The personal pronoun can also be used as an appositive to modify a noun. For example,

> **We** girls like to meet for our coffee break.
> We will let **you** boys go to the football game.

Indefinite Pronouns
Some pronouns refer to people or things in general. These pronouns are called indefinite pronouns. They function in the place of nouns.

> singular indefinite pronouns:
>
>> another, anything, either, everything, no one, somebody, anybody, one, neither, someone, anyone, each, nobody
>
> singular or plural indefinite pronouns:
>
>> everyone, everybody, some, none, any, most

Pronouns Used as Intensifiers
Pronouns may also be used with nouns to intensify them. For example,

> The mayor **himself** gave the order.
> I **myself** did it.

The following pronouns act as intensifiers:

	singular	plural
1st person:	myself	ourselves
2nd person:	yourself	yourselves
3rd person:	himself, herself, itself	themselves

These pronouns may also function by themselves as direct objects. For example,

> She cut **herself** opening the can.
> He threw **himself** against the door.

Relative Pronouns
Many grammarians do not refer to "relative pronouns," considering them merely as subordinators. It is irrelevant how they are classified as long as they are used correctly. Relative pronouns can be used in three ways: they can stand in place of their antecedents (the words to which they refer); they can introduce adjective and noun clauses; and they can introduce questions. The relative pronouns are "who," "which," and "that."

The form "who" is inflected:

> who   (subject form)
> whose   (possessive form)
> whom   (object form)

"Who," "whose," and "whom" refer mainly to people. "Which" refers mainly to things, and "that" refers mainly to things but can also refer to people. (Notice that "what" is not a relative pronoun.)

Relative pronouns with antecedents. When a relative pronoun is used with an antecedent it always takes the same form as the noun to which it is related. For example,

> The boy **who** was late for class   (subject, refers to "boy")
> The boy **whose** rabbit escaped   (possessive, refers to "rabbit" which belongs to the boy)
> The boy of **whom** you spoke.   (object of the verb "spoke," refers to "boy")

Relative pronouns used to introduce clauses. Relative pronouns can also be used to introduce adjective and noun clauses. When they do this, they act as connectives. The use of the pronoun within the clause determines its form. For example,

He wanted to know **whom** the principal had chosen.	(noun clause: "whom" is the object of the verb "had chosen" within the clause)
John is the boy **whom** you must ask.	(adjective clause: "whom" is the object of the verb "must ask" within the clause)
He never discovered **who** was the culprit.	(noun clause: "who" is the subject of the linking-verb "was" within the clause)
This is the man about **whom** I was telling you.	("whom" is the object of the preposition "about" within the clause)

Relative pronouns used to introduce questions. The relative pronouns "who" and "whom" are also used to introduce questions. As in subordination, the form of the pronoun is determined by its function in the sentence. For example,

Who was that girl you were speaking to?	("who" is the subject of the verb "was")
Whom are you looking for?	("whom" is the object of the preposition "for")
Who did you say was outside?	("who" is the subject of the verb "was")
Whom was he fighting?	("whom" is the object of the verb "fighting")

Chapter Three
The Forms of Words

The Characteristics of Words

In the previous chapter we learned that there are five classes of words, each of which has its own particular functions within the sentence. In this chapter we will study the word classes in terms of their unique structural features. Before we do this, however, let us examine the structural characteristics of words in general.

A word is made up of *syllables*. A syllable is built around a single vowel sound, which can be made up of a single vowel, as in "cat," or a combination of vowels, as in "receive," "thought," and "meal." For example, "cát" has one syllable, "énter" has two syllables, "mónkeys" has two syllables, "re-énter" has three syllables, and "ímmédïátélý" has six syllables. A word, therefore, has as many syllables as it has vowel sounds.

Words also consist of *morphemes*. A morpheme is the smallest unit of meaning. For example, "cat," "boy," "horse," and "monkey" are all morphemes.

A morpheme is sometimes the same as a syllable. For example, "cat" and "boy" are both one-syllable words and contain only one morpheme. On the other hand, a morpheme is not necessarily the same as a syllable. For example, "cats" and "boys" are still one-syllable words, but each contains two morphemes. "Cat" and "boy" refer to one special type of animal and one special type of person; each has only one meaning. "Cats" and "boys" refer to a special type of animal and a special type of person, but the addition of -*s* makes each refer also to more than one; each therefore has two meanings. The *plural morpheme,* as this is called, is not always indicated by an additional ending—for example, "mice," "teeth," "children," and "women."

There are three important types of morphemes: (1) base morphemes, (2) derivational morphemes, and (3) inflectional morphemes.

Base morphemes are the simple base words that contain only one unit of meaning, although they may contain more than one syllable. For example, "rain," "dog," "table," "child," "mouse," "tiger."

Derivational morphemes convert a word from one class to another. For example, adding the morpheme *-en* to "wood" makes the original word, a noun, into an adjective, "wooden." Adding the morpheme *-er* to the verb "drive" makes it into the noun "driver." Usually derivational morphemes are *suffixes* (added at the end of a word), although some are *prefixes* (added at the beginning of a word). For example, adding the morpheme *be-* to the adjective "little" turns it into the verb "belittle."

Inflectional morphemes give a word the meaning of some grammatical category such as number or tense. For example, to make a word plural, add the morpheme *-s* (or *-es*). To indicate possession, add the morpheme *-s* and/or an apostrophe. To indicate comparative degrees, add the morphemes *-er* and *-est.* To indicate the past tense, add the morpheme *-ed;* to indicate the present participle, add the morpheme *-ing.* Sometimes more than one morpheme is added to a base word—for example, "teach" + *-er* + *-s* = "teachers" (three morphemes).

Words in general therefore have certain structural patterns: they are made up of syllables; they are made up of morphemes; they are made up of bases to which prefixes and suffixes may be attached. Visualizing words in terms of their basic patterns is helpful in learning to recognize and spell them easily, and in pronouncing and using them effectively.

The Forms of the Word Classes

Each of the four classes of content words has certain characteristics which distinguish the words in that class from the words in the other classes. Most function words, on the other hand, do not have distinctive characteristics by which they may be identified; in fact, a function word often changes its form as it changes its function within a sentence. Because their forms and functions are so closely related, the section on "The Functions of Function Words" in the previous chapter serves also as an analysis of the of the forms of these words. In this section we will examine the distinctive structural features of the four content word classes.

The Form of Nouns

Nouns have five distinctive characteristics that make them different from the other word classes:

1. nouns are inflected to show the plural;
2. nouns are inflected to show the possessive case;
3. nouns have certain characteristic suffixes;
4. certain nouns are capitalized;
5. nouns are pronounced in certain ways.

Inflection to Show the Plural

Nouns may be singular (referring to one) or plural (referring to more than one). They change from the singular to the plural through the addition of an inflectional morpheme. In most cases, this inflectional morpheme is -s. For example,

house	houses
boot	boots
shoe	shoes

Unfortunately, however, there are various other ways of making a singular noun plural. For example, words ending in the sounds /s/, /sh/, /ch/, /ks/ and /z/ add -es to form the plural. For example,

kiss	kisses
witch	witches

fox	foxes
wish	wishes
quiz	quizzes

Notice that words ending in "z" double the final letter before adding -es.

Nouns ending in "y" preceded by a consonant form the plural by changing the "y" to "i" and adding -es.

city	cities
baby	babies
fly	flies
army	armies

Nouns ending in "o" usually form the plural by adding -es.

tomato	tomatoes
potato	potatoes
negro	negroes
hero	heroes

However, some words ending in "o" form the plural merely by adding -s, while others may add either -s or -es.

auto	autos	
radio	radios	
banjo	banjos	banjoes
motto	mottos	mottoes

Nouns ending in "f" or "fe" usually form the plural by changing the "f" to "v" and adding -s or -es.

loaf	loaves
calf	calves
leaf	leaves
wife	wives

However, some words ending in "f" form the plural merely by adding -s, while others may either add -s or change the "f" to "v" and add -es.

    chief   chiefs
    belief   beliefs
    roof   roofs   rooves
    beef   beefs   beeves

Some nouns form the plural by undergoing a vowel change. For example,

    man   men
    foot   feet
    tooth   teeth
    mouse   mice

Some nouns form the plural by adding -en. For example,

    child   children
    brother   brethren
    ox   oxen

Notice how the spelling also changes in the first two examples.

Some nouns, inherited from other languages, retain their foreign plurals.

    alumna   alumnae
    analysis   analyses
    stimulus   stimuli

Some nouns inherited from other languages may take either their foreign plurals or English plurals.

    curriculum   curricula   curriculums
    formula   formulae   formulas
    appendix   appendices appendixes

Some nouns have the same form in both the singular and plural. For example, "deer," "moose," "salmon," "sheep," "cattle."

Some nouns have no means of indicating the plural. For example, "peace," "solitude," "contentment," "anger," "gold," "money."

Some nouns end in "s" but are always used in the singular. For example, "news," "mathematics," "mumps," "summons."

Some nouns ending in "s" are always used in the plural. For example, "wages," "clothes," "shorts," "trousers," "scissors," "pliers."

Compound nouns usually inflect the headword in the compound.

daughter-in-law	daughters-in-law
passerby	passersby
man of war	men of war
round of beef	rounds of beef

Some compound nouns, however, inflect the last part of the compound.

cross-examination	cross-examinations

Inflection to Show the Possessive

The possessive case indicates possession or a close relationship between nouns. In most instances, the possessive can be changed to an "of" prepositional phrase. For example, "Joan's hat" can also be expressed as "the hat of Joan." "The man's remarkable stupidity resulted in an hour's delay" can be expressed as "the remarkable stupidity of the man resulted in a delay of an hour."

The possessive is usually formed by adding an apostrophe and -s (-'s) to the noun. For example, "Joan's hat," "the man's stupidity," "an hour's delay," "women's," "passerby's," "sheep's," "children's." When the noun already ends in "s" only an apostrophe is added.

boss   boss'
dogs   dogs'
witches   witches'
heroes   heroes'

Characteristic Noun Suffixes

These suffixes are derivational morphemes; they indicate that the words to which they are attached may function as nouns. The following list contains some of the most common noun suffixes.

noun suffix	examples	meaning
-acy	accuracy, fallacy, piracy	quality, state, or condition (of being accurate, of being fallacious, etc.)
-ade	blockade, cavalcade, crusade	instance of action
-age	bondage, cartage, orphanage	state or condition; action or process; place for
-al	arrival, rehearsal, denial	instance of action or process
-an -ean -ian	American, Anglican, partisan European, epicurean librarian, Albanian, technician	one belonging to or related to; one skilled in or specializing in
-ance -ence	attendance, furtherance, protuberance emergence, reference, correspondence	instance of action or process; quality or state; amount or degree

noun suffix	examples	meaning
-ancy	piquancy, buoyancy, expectancy	quality or state
-ency	emergency, despondency, dependency, presidency	
-ant	servant, accountant, pendant	that which is; one who is or does
-ent	serpent, correspondent	
-ary	library, budgetary, functionary	connected with or belonging to; place for; quality or condition; practice of
-ery	slavery, finery, bakery cookery	
-ry	wizardry, citizenry, heraldry	
-dom	kingdom, freedom, Christendom	state of being; geographical area; realm of jurisdiction
-ee	employee, emcee goatee, bargee	who who is or does; that which is associated with
-eer	auctioneer, pioneer profiteer	one who is or does; that which is or does
-er	worker, painter, teacher	
-ess	actress, countess, giantess	
-or	actor, editor, sculptor	
-ful	cupful, roomful, handful	number or quantity that fills or would fill
-hood	manhood, statehood falsehood	condition, state, or quality

noun suffix	examples	meaning
-ia	phobia, paraphernalia, saturnalia	derived from or related to
-ic	phobic, paralytic, alcoholic	one having the nature of or one affected by
-ion -tion	tension, explosion, repulsion resolution, tradition, solution	act, process, or condition; result of an act, process, or condition
-ism	communism, capitalism, sonambulism	act, practice, or process of; doctrine or theory of
-ist	communist, typist, dentist	one who is or does; one related to or associated with
-ity	calamity, salinity, probity	state, condition, or quality
-let	booklet, pamphlet, piglet	small in size
-ment	resentment, contentment, apartment	state or condition; place for
-ness	kindness, goodness, quickness	state, condition, or quality
-ship	friendship, relationship, sportsmanship	state, condition, or quality
-sis	paralysis, ellipsis, parenthesis	process or action; result of a process or action

noun suffix	examples	meaning
-th	warmth, dearth, health	state or condition
-ure	manicure, sinecure, legislature	act or process; office or function; person or group performing action
-y	monarchy, inquiry, soldiery, haberdashery	instance of action; quality or condition; body or group; place for

Capitalization of Certain Nouns

Certain nouns that name particular persons and things are capitalized. For example,

> people: John Brown, Mary Poppins
> titles: President Johnson, Prince Philip, Madame Curé
> ship names, brand names, etc.: the *Titanic,* Mustang
> places: Los Angeles, America, Southeast Asia
> races: Caucasian, Oriental
> organizations and institutions: the Boy Scouts, Harvard University, Hillmead School
> special events and times: the Olympic Games, the Renaissance
> the Deity: God, Allah, Our Lord
> documents and publications: the Magna Carta, *Life* magazine, *The Grapes of Wrath,* "The Waste Land"
> months, days of the week, holidays: June, Monday, Lincoln's Birthday

Identification by Stress

Nouns can usually be identified in conversation by the position of the stress given to them. If you say the following words aloud, using them first as nouns and then as verbs, you will notice that you put a stress on the first part of the words when you use them as nouns, and a stress on the second part when you use them as verbs.

nouns	verbs
áddress	addréss
cómpound	compóund
cóncert	concért
cónduct	condúct
órder	ordér
récord	recórd
súbject	subjéct
súspect	suspéct

In summary, nouns can be identified by inflectional endings, by characteristic suffixes, sometimes by capitalization, and, in conversation, by stress. Nouns can also be recognized by their functions and positions in sentences and by the presence of certain signal words. Finally, here is one last method for the recognition of nouns: if a word added to the following framework completes its sense, it is a noun.

I was thinking of _____.

I was thinking of my husband.	(noun)
I was thinking until.	(not a noun)
I was thinking of your advice.	(noun)

The Forms of Verbs

Verbs have four distinctive characteristics that make them different from the other word classes:

1. verbs have certain inflectional changes which indicate number and tense;
2. verbs have certain characteristic prefixes;
3. verbs have certain characteristic suffixes;
4. verbs are pronounced in certain ways.

The Forms of Words

Inflectional Changes

As we saw in the previous chapter on the functions of words, verbs may be divided into four-part regular verbs and five-part, four-part, and three-part irregular verbs according to the ways in which they are inflected.

The inflection of regular verbs. Most verbs can change their simple or infinitive form in four ways—that is, they have four "inflected" forms. Verbs with these four inflected forms are called *regular* verbs.

Three of the four forms indicate *tense:* the simple or infinitive ("walk"), the past (formed by adding the morpheme *-ed* to the infinitive—"walked"), and the present participle (formed by adding the morpheme *-ing* to the infinitive—"walking").

The fourth form indicates *number:* the third person singular in the present tense (formed by adding the morpheme *-s* to the infinitive). Verbs show a difference in form to indicate number (singular or plural) only in the third person singular and only in the present tense. The verb "to be" is the one exception: the second person singular always takes the plural form of the verb. Notice also how the verb "to be" changes in the past tense as well as in the present.

	singular	**plural**
present:	I am	we are
	you are	you are
	he is	they are
past:	I was	we were
	you were	you were
	he was	they were

Here are some examples of the four forms of regular verbs:

infinitive	past	present participle	third person singular in the present tense
(to) stay	stayed	staying	stays

infinitive	past	present participle	third person singular in the present tense
(to) jump	jumped	jumping	jumps
(to) move	moved	moving	moves
(to) hurry	hurried	hurrying	hurries
(to) wish	wished	wishing	wishes
(to) equip	equipped	equipping	equips

Notice the spelling changes in the last three examples. Notice also that when a simple form ends in "y," the "y" is changed to "i" before -ed is added to form the past, and -es is added instead of -s to form the third person singular in the present tense. This is also the case with verbs ending in "s," "sc," "ch," and "sh" (see "wishes"). Verbs of one syllable (or more than one, if the final syllable is accented) which end with a consonant preceded by a single vowel ("clip," "equip") double the final consonant when adding -ed or -ing to form the past and present participle.

The inflection of irregular verbs. Unfortunately, not all verbs follow the same inflectional forms as those outlined above. Verbs showing variations in these forms are called *irregular* verbs.

The most commonly used, and most irregular, of the irregular verbs are "to be" and "to have." These two verbs, which are often combined with other verbs, not only change tense forms irregularly but also change from person to person in the present tense. The forms of the verbs "to be" and "to have":

infinitive	past	present participle
be	been	being
have	had	having

The present tense:

    I am, he is, we are, you are, they are
    I have, he has, we have, you have, they have

The following are examples of the verbs "to be" and "to have" used as main verbs:

I **am** the luckiest girl alive.
Joan **is** the nicest girl I know.
The boy **was** very handsome.
The birds **were** black and yellow.

The voyage **will be** pleasant.

The voyage **has been** pleasant.

I **have** a new dress.
Joan **has** a new hat.
The boy **has had** a cold.
The medicine **had had** a terrible effect.
The voyage **will have** to be short.
The baby **is having** a nap.

The following are examples of the verbs "to be" and "to have" used as auxiliary verbs:

I **am** working late tonight.
He **has been** gardening all day.

The young man **was being** led astray.

I **have** to go home.
He **has come** to do the gardening.
The old man **had intended** to leave.

    The chief characteristic of irregular verbs is that they do not add *-ed* to form the past tense. Sometimes the change from the infinitive to the past involves the change of the internal vowel, as in "write–wrote," "sit–sat," "come–came." Sometimes, however, a completely "new" word is used, as in "catch–caught," "fly–flew," "go–went."

    The change in form results from the early German derivations of our language. In old English, verbs were divided into the "strong" and the "weak." The "strong" verbs indicated changes in tense by changes in their internal vowels. For example,

	infinitive	past	past participle
Old English:	etan	œt, œton	eten
English:	eat	ate	eaten

	infinitive	past	past participle
Old English:	binden, bindan	band, bunden	bunden, gebunden
English:	bind	bound	bound

The "weak" verbs indicated the past tense by using suffixes. These suffixes were *-de, -ode,* and *-te.* For example,

	infinitive	past
Old English:	dēman	dēmde
English:	deem	deemed
Old English:	lōcian	lōcode
English:	look	looked
Old English:	sēcan	sōhte
English:	seek	sought

Five-part irregular verbs. These verbs have five inflected forms because their past participles differ from their simple past forms. There are approximately 50 five-part irregular verbs. Notice that several have two acceptable forms in the past participle.

infinitive	past	present participle	past participle	third person singular in the present tense
bear	bore	bearing	born (borne)	bears
begin	began	beginning	begun	begins
bite	bit	biting	bitten	bites
blow	blew	blowing	blown	blows
break	broke	breaking	broken	breaks
choose	chose	choosing	chosen	chooses
do	did	doing	done	does
draw	drew	drawing	drawn	draws
drive	drove	driving	driven	drives
drink	drank	drinking	drunk	drinks
eat	ate	eating	eaten	eats
fall	fell	falling	fallen	falls

infinitive	past	present participle	past participle	third person singular in the present tense
fly	flew	flying	flown	flies
forbid	forbade (forbad)	forbidding	forbidden	forbids
forget	forgot	forgetting	forgotten (forgot)	forgets
forsake	forsook	forsaking	forsaken	forsakes
freeze	froze	freezing	frozen	freezes
get	got	getting	got (gotten)	gets
give	gave	giving	given	gives
go	went	going	gone	goes
grow	grew	growing	grown	grows
hide	hid	hiding	hidden	hides
know	knew	knowing	known	knows
lie	lay	lying	lain	lies
ride	rode	riding	ridden	rides
ring	rang	ringing	rung	rings
rise	rose	rising	risen	rises
see	saw	seeing	seen	sees
shake	shook	shaking	shaken	shakes
shrink	shrank	shrinking	shrunk	shrinks
sing	sang	singing	sung	sings
sink	sank	sinking	sunk	sinks
slay	slew	slaying	slain	slays
smite	smote	smiting	smitten	smites
speak	spoke	speaking	spoken	speaks
spring	sprang	springing	sprung	springs
steal	stole	stealing	stolen	steals
stink	stank	stinking	stunk	stinks
stride	strode	striding	stridden	strides
strive	strove	striving	striven	strives
swear	swore	swearing	sworn	swears
swim	swam	swimming	swum	swims
take	took	taking	taken	takes

infinitive	past	present participle	past participle	third person singular in the present tense
tear	tore	tearing	torn	tears
throw	threw	throwing	thrown	throws
tread	trod	treading	trodden	treads
wear	wore	wearing	worn	wears
weave	wove	weaving	woven	weaves
write	wrote	writing	written	writes

Four-part irregular verbs. These verbs have four forms like the regular verbs. They differ from regular verbs in that they do not add the morpheme *-ed* to indicate the past, but instead take on a variety of forms. They do not have a special past participle like the five-part irregular verbs. There are approximately 60 of these verbs, although some of them can be counted as regular verbs because of alternate past forms.

infinitive	past	present participle	third person singular in the present tense
abide	abode (abided)	abiding	abides
behold	beheld	beholding	beholds
bend	bent	bending	bends
bereave	bereft (bereaved)	bereaving	bereaves
beseech	besought (beseeched)	beseeching	beseeches
bind	bound	binding	binds
bleed	bled	bleeding	bleeds
breed	bred	breeding	breeds
bring	brought	bringing	brings
build	built	building	builds
buy	bought	buying	buys
catch	caught	catching	catches
cling	clung	clinging	clings

infinitive	past	present participle	third person singular in the present tense
clothe	clad (clothed)	clothing	clothes
creep	crept	creeping	creeps
deal	dealt	dealing	deals
dream	dreamt	dreaming	dreams
dwell	dwelt (dwelled)	dwelling	dwells
feed	fed	feeding	feeds
feel	felt	feeling	feels
fight	fought	fighting	fights
find	found	finding	finds
flee	fled	fleeing	flees
fling	flung	flinging	flings
grind	ground	grinding	grinds
hang	hung (hanged)	hanging	hangs
have	had	having	has
hear	heard	hearing	hears
heave	hove (heaved)	heaving	heaves
hold	held	holding	holds
keep	kept	keeping	keeps
kneel	knelt (kneeled)	kneeling	kneels
lay	laid	laying	lays
lead	led	leading	leads
leap	leapt (leaped)	leaping	leaps
learn	learnt (learned)	learning	learns
leave	left	leaving	leaves
lend	lent	lending	lends
light	lit (lighted)	lighting	lights
lose	lost	losing	loses
make	made	making	makes
mean	meant	meaning	means
meet	met	meeting	meets
pay	paid	paying	pays
say	said	saying	says
seek	sought	seeking	seeks

infinitive	past	present participle	third person singular in the present tense
sell	sold	selling	sells
shine	shone (shined)	shining	shines
shoe	shod (shoed)	shoeing	shoes
shoot	shot	shooting	shoots
sit	sat	sitting	sits
sleep	slept	sleeping	sleeps
sling	slung	slinging	slings
slink	slunk	slinking	slinks
speed	sped (speeded)	speeding	speeds
spend	spent	spending	spends
spill	spilt (spilled)	spilling	spills
spin	spun	spinning	spins
stand	stood	standing	stands
stick	stuck	sticking	sticks
sting	stung	stinging	stings
strike	struck	striking	strikes
string	strung	stringing	strings
sweep	swept	sweeping	sweeps
swing	swung	swinging	swings
teach	taught	teaching	teaches
tell	told	telling	tells
think	thought	thinking	thinks
thrive	throve (thrived)	thriving	thrives
wake	woke (waked)	waking	wakes
weep	wept	weeping	weeps
win	won	winning	wins
wind	wound (winded)	winding	winds
wring	wrung	wringing	wrings

The verbs "to come" and "to run" vary from the rest of the four-part irregular verbs because the infinitive form rather than the past form is used as the past participle.

infinitive	past	present participle	past participle
come	came	coming	(has) come
run	ran	running	(has) run

The verb "to read" is also considered a four-part verb rather than a three-part verb because of its variance in pronounciation.

infinitive	past	present participle	third person singular in the present tense
read (rēd)	read (rĕd)	reading	reads

Three-part irregular verbs. These verbs are the easiest to learn because they do not have special forms for the past. There are approximately 20, although some of them could be considered regular verbs because of alternate past forms.

infinitive	past	present participle	third person singular in the present tense
beat	beat (beaten)	beating	beats
bet	bet (betted)	betting	bets
burst	burst (bursted)	bursting	bursts
cast	cast	casting	casts
cost	cost	costing	costs
cut	cut	cutting	cuts
hit	hit	hitting	hits
hurt	hurt	hurting	hurts
let	let	letting	lets
put	put	putting	puts
rid	rid	ridding	rids
set	set	setting	sets
shed	shed	shedding	sheds
shut	shut	shutting	shuts

102   A Short Guide to the New Grammar

infinitive	past	present participle	third person singular in the present tense
slit	slit	slitting	slits
split	split	splitting	splits
spread	spread	spreading	spreads
thrust	thrust	thrusting	thrusts
wed	wed	wedding	weds
wet	wet	wetting	wets

Some additional comments on the irregular forms of verbs may be helpful for correct spelling and usage.

Some irregular verbs add *-n* or *-en* to the past form to make the past participle. (Notice also how their spellings change to form the past.)

infinitive	past	past participle
bear	bore	borne
beat	beat	beaten
bite	bit	bitten
break	broke	broken
choose	chose	chosen
freeze	froze	frozen
speak	spoke	spoken
steal	stole	stolen
swear	swore	sworn
tear	tore	torn
wear	wore	worn

Some irregular verbs change the middle vowel from "i" in the infinitive form to "a" in the past form, and to "u" in the past participle.

infinitive	past	past participle
begin	began	begun

infinitive	past	past participle
drink	drank	drunk
ring	rang	rung
sing	sang	sung
sink	sank (sunk)	sunk
spring	sprang (sprung)	sprung
swim	swam	swum

Some irregular verbs make the past participle from the infinitive form rather than from the past form.

infinitive	past	past participle
blow	blew	blown
come	came	come
do	did	done
draw	drew	drawn
eat	ate	eaten
fall	fell	fallen
give	gave	given
go	went	gone
grow	grew	grown
know	knew	known
ride	rode	ridden
rise	rose	risen
run	ran	run
see	saw	seen
shake	shook	shaken
slay	slew	slain
take	took	taken
throw	threw	thrown
write	wrote	written

Characteristic Verb Prefixes
A verb can sometimes be identified by its prefix. The following

list contains some characteristic verb prefixes.

verb prefix	examples	meaning
ab-	abscond, abdicate, abstract	from, away
ad-	adhere, advise, adapt	to, towards, before, near
af-	affix, affect, affiance	
ag-	aggrandize, aggravate	
al-	allege, allay, alleviate	
ap-	approximate, apply, appreciate	
as-	assuage, assume, associate	
at-	attain, attract, attribute	
be-	belittle, bewitch, become	to do
co-	cohese, coordinate, coexist	with
de-	defrost, decapitate, descend	from, away, down
em-	embitter, embark, empower	cause to be; provide with; place in
en-	encase, enthrone, entangle	
il-	illuminate, illustrate	in, within, into, toward
im-	impress, imply, immerse	
in-	incline, incite, incur	
ir-	irradiate, irritate, irrigate	
inter-	intervene, intermingle	between
pro-	proceed, produce, procrastinate	forward
re-	retreat, reimburse, remake	again
sub-	subtract, subsidize, subside	under

verb prefix	examples	meaning
trans-	transport, translate, transfer	across
un-	undo, unable, unhand	not
with-	withstand, withdraw, withhold	back from

Characteristic Verb Suffixes

Verbs also have certain characteristic suffixes; examples are given in the following list.

verb suffixes	examples	meaning
-ate	placate, officiate, negotiate	to make or do
-en	brighten, sharpen, quicken	to make or do
-fy	magnify, classify, satisfy	to make or do
-ize	idolize, rationalize, commercialize	to make like

Identification by Stress

Verbs, like nouns, can sometimes be identified in conversation by the position of the stress given to them. Verbs of two syllables are commonly accented on the final syllable. Examples of this are given on page 92.

In summary, verbs can be identified by inflectional endings, characteristic prefixes and suffixes, and by the stress given to them in conversation. Verbs, like nouns, can also be identified by their functions and positions within sentences and by the presence of certain signal words. Here is one last method for recognizing verbs: if a word can be placed in the following framework, it is a verb.

They might _____ them.

The Form of Adjectives

Adjectives have two distinctive characteristics that make them different from the other word classes:

    1. adjectives are inflected to show degrees of comparison;
    2. adjectives have certain characteristic suffixes.

Inflection to Show Comparison

Nearly all one-syllable adjectives, and a few with two syllables, may be inflected by adding the derivational morphemes *-er* to form the comparative and *-est* to form the superlative. For example,

simple form	comparative	superlative
young	younger	youngest
fine	finer	finest
hot	hotter	hottest
hard	harder	hardest
warm	warmer	warmest
wise	wiser	wisest
healthy	healthier	healthiest
happy	happier	happiest
might	mightier	mightiest

Some are inflected irregularly. For example,

simple form	comparative	superlative
bad	worse	worst
far	farther (further)	farthest (furthest)
many	more	most
good	better	best
little	less	least

Nearly all other adjectives use "more" or "less" to form the comparative, and "most" or "least" to form the superlative.

simple form	comparative	superlative
hopeful	more hopeful	most hopeful
flexible	more flexible	most flexible
suitable	less suitable	least suitable
careful	less careful	least careful

When "more," "less," "most," and "least" are used to indicate degrees of comparison, they function as intensifiers, as do such words as "very," "really," "rather," and "particularly," which can also be used with adjectives to show degree.

Characteristic Adjective Suffixes

These suffixes are derivational morphemes that convert a base word (usually a noun or verb) into an adjective. They include the following:

suffix	examples
-able	lovable, comfortable
-al	personal, musical
-an	American, suburban
-ant	important, sonant
-ar	linear, nuclear
-ary,	revolutionary, reactionary
-ate	ornate, fortunate
-ed	cultured, ragged
-en	wooden, earthen
-ent	dependent, excellent
-ful	beautiful, bountiful
-ic	historic, allergic
-ical	historical, comical
-ile	servile, juvenile
-ish	foolish, impish
-ive	uncommunicative, attentive
-less	hopeless, fearless

suffix	examples
-like	lifelike, ladylike
-ly	stately, kindly
-ory	introductory, ambulatory
-ous, -ious	joyous, delicious
-y	jolly, surly

The Form of Adverbs

Adverbs are the most difficult words to classify because they function in a variety of ways and are often similar in form to the other word classes. However, there are three particular characteristics in their structure that help us to identify them:

1. adverbs are inflected to show degrees of comparison;
2. adverbs have a certain characteristic prefix;
3. adverbs have certain characteristic suffixes.

Inflection to Show Comparison

Adverbs are similar to adjectives in that they can be inflected to show comparative and superlative degrees. One-syllable adverbs, like one-syllable adjectives, do this by adding the derivational morphemes *-er* and *-est*. For example,

simple form	comparative	superlative
early	earlier	earliest
hard	harder	hardest
near	nearer	nearest
long	longer	longest
far	farther	farthest
fast	faster	fastest

Notice how many of the above examples may also be used as adjectives. Again, like adjectives, adverbs of more than one syllable are inflected to show comparative degrees by using the intensifiers "more," "most," "less," and "least."

simple form	comparative	superlative
beautifully	more beautifully	most beautifully
cautiously	more cautiously	most cautiously

Some adverbs are inflected irregularly. For example,

simple form	comparative	superlative
badly	worse	worst
far	farther (further)	farthest (furthest)
little	less	least
much	more	most
well	better	best

Characteristic Adverb Prefix
Adverbs can often be recognized by the characteristic prefix *a-*. For example, "across," "aboard," "abreast," "ahead," "aground," "away," "apart," "adrift," "anew."

Characteristic Adverb Suffixes
The addition of the derivational morpheme *-ly* turns many adjectives into adverbs. For example,

merry	merrily
hopeful	hopefully
attentive	attentively
separate	separately
careless	carelessly

Adverbs can also be formed from nouns through the addition of the morpheme *-ly*.

day	daily
month	monthly
night	nightly

The following list contains other characteristic adverb suffixes:

suffix	examples
-how	somehow, anyhow
-long	headlong, sidelong
-most	uppermost, innermost
-side	inside, alongside
-time	sometime, anytime
-ward	backward, forward
-way	anyway, straightaway
-where	somewhere, anywhere
-wise	clockwise, crabwise

In summary, adverbs are the most difficult class of content words to identify. A large number of them have no characteristic formal elements. For example,

almost	soon	back
already	often	forth
ever	always	here
never	also	there
now	even	near
then	instead	north
yesterday	yet	south
tomorrow	thus	

Also, many of the words we commonly think of as adverbs are actually function words (prepositions) used as verb modifiers: "about," "above," "after," "before," "behind," "below," "by," "in," "over," "through," and so on.

Some adverbs may be identified by placing the words "more," "less," "most," and "least" in front of them to see if they make sense. This, however, applies also to adjectives. Adverbs are often difficult to distinguish from adjectives; in some cases the forms of the words are similar, and both classes share the modifying function. There are two ways in which adjectives may be differentiated from adverbs: (1) adjectives are usually essential to the structure and meaning of the sentence pattern, and (2) adjectives usually modify only one word in the sentence.

noun	verb	noun	adjective
She	acted		suspicious.
The man	hit	the ball	wild.

The words "suspicious" and "wild" modify the nouns "she" and "the man." They are, therefore, adjectives. Notice also how they form part of the predicate and are needed to complete the sense of the sentence. In contrast to adjectives, (1) adverbs are not usually essential to the structure and meaning of the sentence, and (2) adverbs usually relate to the whole situation or to the complete sentence.

noun	verb	noun	adverb
She	acted		suspicously.
The man	hit	the ball	wildly.

In these examples, "suspiciously" and "wildly" modify the verbs "acted" and "hit," but they are not necessary to the basic structures or meanings of the sentences.

Finally, two frameworks can be used to distinguish some adverbs and adjectives. If a word fits into the following framework, it is an adjective.

>   They seem _____. (happy, slow, cautious, etc.)

If a word fits into the following framework, it is an adverb.

>   They did it _____. (happily, slowly, cautiously, etc.)

The Formation of Words

We have discussed the ways in which the form of a word can indicate its class and function. In this section we will see how the form of a word can also help us to understand its meaning.

For example, a knowledge of the separate parts of the word "transportation" would enable us to decipher its meaning even if we had never met the whole word before: "trans" means "across"; "port" means "to carry"; and thus "transportation" means something to do with "carrying across." *Trans-* is the prefix of the word because it comes before the word root; "port" is the root or base because it is the basic element of the word to which the other parts are attached; and *-ation* is the suffix because it is added to the end of the word root.

Notice how the addition of prefixes and suffixes (collectively called *affixes*) can change the meaning of the word root "port":

prefix	root	suffix	meaning
trans-	port		to carry across
de-	port		to carry (away) from
	port	*-able*	can be carried
im-	port		to carry into
ex-	port		to carry out of
re-	port		to carry back
	port	*-er*	one who carries

In the following examples, notice how the function and meaning of the word root "spect" ("to look") is affected by affixes:

prefix	root	suffix	meaning
re-	spect		to look back, has come to mean to esteem, honor, or give particular at-

prefix	root	suffix	meaning
			tention to (verb); esteem, honor, or particular attention (noun)
in-	spect		to look into (verb)
in-	spect	-or	one who looks into (noun)
su(b)-	spect	to look up	to look up at, has come to mean to look at with doubt or distrust (verb); one who is looked at with doubt or distrust (noun)
	spect	-acle	something to look at (noun)
	spect	-ator	one who looks at (noun)

An analysis of word elements (prefixes, word roots, and suffixes) shows very clearly the influence of Greek and Latin upon our language. We will now examine some of the elements we have "borrowed" from these sources in order to understand better the formation of words.

Prefixes

The following prefixes were acquired from Latin:

prefix	meaning	example	meaning
a-, ab-	from, away, not	atypical	not typical
ad-	to, toward	adapt	to fit to
ante-	before	anteroom	room that comes before another room

prefix	meaning	example	meaning
anti-	against	antitoxin	substance that acts against a toxic substance
auto-	self	automobile	moves by itself
bi-	two	bicycle	a two-wheeler
co-	with	cooperate	to work together
de-	from, away	defrost	to free from frost
dis-	lack of, apart	discomfort	lack of comfort
e-, ex-	out of	exit	a place to go out
in-	not	incomplete	not complete
inter-	between	international	between nations
intra-	within	intramural	within the walls (of an institution or group)
mis-	wrong	misspent	spent wrongly or foolishly
post-	after	postscript	written after the main part of something
pro-	forward	produce	bring forward
re-	back	retrace	trace back
semi-	half	semicircle	a half circle
sub-	under, up	submarine	under the sea
super-	beyond	supernatural	beyond the natural
trans-	across	transport	to carry across

Several prefixes mean "not" or "the opposite of": *un-, in-, im-, il-, ir-,* and *mis-*. When these prefixes are added to the beginning of a word they reverse its meaning. For example, the antonym (opposite) of "happy" is "unhappy"; the antonym of "fortune" is "misfortune."

The following Greek prefixes are found in many English words as well as in words of other languages:

prefix	meaning	prefix	meaning
a-	not	*micro-*	small
anti-	against	*neo-*	new
arch-	chief	*ortho-*	straight
auto-	self	*pan-*	all
em-, en-	in	*para-*	beside
epi-	on top	*peri-*	around
hemi-	half	*poly-*	many
hetero-	different	*pro-*	before
homo-	same	*pseudo-*	false
hyper-	above	*syn-*	together
hypo-	under	*tele-*	far, distant

Sometimes the original forms of the Latin and Greek prefixes are slightly changed before they are added to the root words. For example, the word "accumulate" does not contain the prefix *ac-* as one might expect, but contains instead an adapted form of *ad-*. These prefix changes usually occur for convenience in pronunciation—it is much easier to say "accumulate" than "adcumulate." The process by which such changes occur is called *assimilation*, the adaption of a sound to an adjacent sound.

ad-

ad+lot = allot
ad+filiate = affiliate
ad+peal = appeal
ad+tain = attain

com-

com+lect = collect
com+cord = concord
com+rupt = corrupt
com+exist = coexist

dis-

dis+fer = differ
dis+ficult = difficult
dis+gest = digest
dis+lute = dilute

ex-

ex+face = efface
ex+fect = effect
ex+lect = elect
ex+rode = erode

in-	*sub-*
in+legal = illegal	sub+ceed = succeed
in+mortal - immortal	sub+fix = suffix
in+regular = irregular	sub+port = support
in+reparable = irreparable	sub+pend = suspend

Additional examples of this process are given in the sections on noun suffixes (page 88) and on verb prefixes (page 104).

The easiest way to analyze words into their correct components is to use a dictionary that indicates the original affixes. For example, if you look up the word "differ," you will find: "L, *differre,* to carry apart, postpone, be different, fr. *dis-* (apart) + *ferre* (to carry)." *Dis-* is the original prefix and "ferre" is the original root.

Word Roots

Usually it is not difficult to identify the prefix of a word. The *un-* of "unclear," the *mis-* of "misfortune," and the *re-* of "return" are all obviously prefixes. It is somewhat more difficult, however, to identify the root of a word.

Word roots occur in two forms: bound and free. *Free forms* are word roots that can appear by themselves, although they can also attach affixes. For example, "true," "turn," and "port." *Bound forms,* on the other hand, cannot stand alone; they always appear with affixes. For example, "clude" ("conclude"), "gress" ("transgress"), and "ceive" ("receive"). Bound or free, the root of a word is its basic element and contains its central meaning.

The following list contains some common Latin word roots:

word root	meaning	example	meaning
fort	strong	fortress	a strong place
cred	to believe	incredible	not believable
tele	far away	television	the transmission of pictures far away

word root	meaning	example	meaning
flect, flex	to bend	reflect	to bend back
pater	father	paternal	associated with the father
equ	even	equalize	to make even
meter	measure	thermometer	heat measurer
ped	foot	pedestrian	one who goes on foot
dic, dict	say, speak	diction	speech
fac, fact	do, make	factory	place where something is made
junct	join	junction	place where something is joined
pon, pos	place, put	deposit	to put into
scrib, script	write	script	written
spect, spic	look, see	spectacle	something to see
tract	draw, pull	traction	pulling
vert, vers	turn	reverse	turn back
voc	call	vocation	a calling
volv	roll, turn	revolve	turn around

The following list contains some common Greek word roots:

word root	meaning	example	meaning
anthro	man	anthropoid	man-like
psycho	mind	psychosomatic	physical illness caused by the mind
hydr	water	hydraulic	operated by force of water
morph	form	amorphous	without form
mon	one	monocle	eye glass for one eye

word root	meaning	example	meaning
pan	all	panorama	an all-encompassing view
gen	birth, race family, production	eugenics	science for improving offspring
phon	voice	phonetic	relating to spoken sounds
geo	earth	geophysicist	one who studies physics of the earth
ortho	straight	orthopedist	one who straightens bones
tele	distant, far away	telepathy	transference of thoughts from far away
chron	time	chronology	arrangement or measurement in time
scope	seeing	horoscope	instrument for seeing into the future
homo	same	homonyms	words with same sound
neo	new	neophyte	a new member

Suffixes

We discussed suffixes in some detail in the earlier part of this chapter when considering the characteristic forms of the word classes. Here is a list of the major suffixes of each word class so that we may compare them:

noun suffix	meaning	example	meaning
-an	one belonging to or related to	American	one belonging to America
-ance, -ence	instance of action or process; quality or state; amount or degree	attendance	instance of action of attending

noun suffix	meaning	example	meaning
-ary, *-ery*	connected with or belonging to; quality or condition of; place for; practice of	library	place for books
-dom	state of being	freedom	state of being free
-hood	condition, state or quality	manhood	state of being a man
-ism	art, practice, or process of	patriotism	act or practice of being patriotic
-ist	one who is or does; one associated with	dentist	one associated with teeth
-ment	state or condition	resentment	state of resenting
-ness	state, condition or quality	kindness	quality of being kind
-or, *-er*	one who is or does	actor	one who acts
-ship	condition, state or quality	friendship	state of being a friend
-tion, *-ion*	act, process, or condition; result of act, process, or condition	civilization	result of process of civilizing

verb suffix	meaning	example	meaning
-ate	to make or do	placate	to make placid
-fy	to make	magnify	to make larger
-ize	to make like	dramatize	to make like drama

adjective suffix	meaning	example	meaning
-able, *-ible*	capacity of being	lovable	capable of being loved
-al	pertaining to, like	royal	pertaining to a king

adjective suffix	meaning	example	meaning
-ary, -ory	pertaining to, like	introductory	pertaining to an introduction
-en	of the nature of	wooden	like wood
-ic	pertaining to, like	comic	pertaining to comedy
-ical	pertaining to, like	historical	pertaining to history
-il, -ile	pertaining to, like	juvenile	like youth
-ish	of the nature of	foolish	like a fool
-less	without	hopeless	without hope
-ous, -ious	full of	joyous	full of joy

adverb suffix	meaning	example	meaning
-er	more (in degree)	shorter	more short
-est	most (in degree)	latest	most late
-ly	manner, like	friendly	like a friend
-most	highest (in degree)	uppermost	highest in position

Chapter Four
The Relationships of Sound to Meaning, Spelling, and Pronunciation

Phonemes and Graphemes: The Symbols of Language
Language conveys our thoughts through symbols. Sounds are the symbols of spoken language and letters are the symbols of written language. It is the way we combine these sounds or letters that makes our communications effective or ineffective.

The basic sounds of language are called *phonemes*. They are the sounds that differentiate meaning. For example, the *c* sound in "cat" and the *b* sound in "bat" are phonemes because they are the elements that give the words two entirely different meanings.

The letters of written language are called *graphemes*. They represent the phonemes. For example, "c" stands for the *c* sound in "cat."

There are approximately 40 different phonemes in the English language. Unfortunately, there are only 26 graphemes, or letters of the alphabet. It is this lack of representative graphemes that makes our language so difficult to master, particularly its spelling and pronunciation.

In this chapter we will see how the 26 letters of the alphabet are used to represent the 43 different sounds of English. As you study the charts below, try to develop a sensitivity to the sound-spelling relationships—this is very helpful in mastering new words. Remember that each phonemic symbol represents only one sound, although each sound may be represented by more than one letter.

The Phonemes and Graphemes of Consonants
There are 24 single consonant phonemes and two combined

consonant phonemes.

The following chart illustrates the phonemic symbols for the consonant sounds. The first column lists the phonemic symbols used by most linguists today. They are shown enclosed in right-slanting lines. These symbols may differ from those given in your dictionary because each dictionary has its own method for indicating sounds. The dictionary symbols closest to those in the chart may be found in *Webster's Seventh New Collegiate Dictionary* (G. and C. Merriam Co., 1963). The symbols in *Webster's* that differ from those in the chart are shown enclosed in left-slanting lines (there are no dictionary symbols for the combined phonemes). The second column lists the graphemes that represent the phonemic sounds and gives examples of each.

phonemic symbol　　**graphemes with examples**

/b/　　*b:* ball, rub; *bb:* rubber; *be:* cube

/ch/ or /č/ \ch\　　*ch:* church; *tch:* ditch; *ti:* convention; *te:* righteous; *t:* lecture; *sci:* conscious; *si:* tension

/d/　　*d:* doll; *dd:* add; *de:* side; *ed:* mobbed

/f/　　*f:* fun; *ff:* cuff; *fe:* life; *ph:* graph; *gh:* rough

/g/　　*g:* girl; *gg:* egg; *gu(e):* fatigue

/h/　　*h:* hat; *wh:* who

/j/ or /ǰ/　　*j:* jet; *g:* gentle; *gg:* exaggerate; *dg(e):* ledge; *ge:* luggage

/k/　　*k:* king; *c:* cold; *cc:* baccalaureate; *ch:* chronology; *ck:* kick; *kē:* like; *qu:* queen; *q:* quick; *cq:* acquaint

The Relationships of Sound

phonemic symbol	graphemes with examples
/l/	*l:* pail; *ll:* pull; *le:* while
/m/	*m:* my; *mm:* swimming; *mb:* limb
/n/	*n:* nut; *nn:* sunny; *gn:* gnome; *kn:* know; *ne:* wine
/ng/ or /ŋ/ \ŋ\	*n:* ink; *ng:* lung; *ngue:* tongue
/p/	*p:* pie; *pp:* happy
/r/	*r:* run; *rr:* carry; *re:* care; *wr:* wrong
/s/	*s:* sun; *ss:* fuss; *se:* base; *sc:* scene; *c:* center; *ce:* mice; *z:* quartz
/sh/ or /š/ \sh\	*sh:* shoe; *s:* sugar; *ss:* tissue; *se:* nauseous; *si:* expulsion; *ssi:* mission; *xi:* anxious; *sch:* schmaltz; *ti:* operation; *ch:* machine; *ce:* ocean; *ci:* malicious
/th/ or /ð/ \th\	*th:* that; *the:* bathe
/t̶h̶/ or /θ/ \th\	*th:* thin
/t/	*t:* ten; *tt:* matter; *te:* late; *ed:* clipped
/v/	*v:* voice; *vv:* flivver; *ve:* live; *f:* of
/w/	*w:* woman; *o:* one; *u:* quick
/y/	*y:* year; *u:* use
/z/	*z:* zoo; *zz:* gizzard; *ze:* sneeze; *s:* is; *se:* rose; *ss:* scissors; *x:* xylophone
/zh/ or /ž/ \zh\	*z:* azure; *g:* garage; *s:* treasure; *si:* explosion

combined phonemes   **graphemes with examples**

/ks/   *x:* box

/gz/   *x:* exist

The Phonemes and Graphemes of Vowels

The following chart illustrates the phonemic symbols for vowel sounds. There are 17 vowel phonemes.

phonemic symbols   **graphemes with examples**

/a/ or /æ/ \a\   *a:* cat; *ai:* plaid

/e/   *e:* red; *a:* many; *u:* bury; *ea:* dead;
                       ai: said; *ei:* heifer; *ie:* friend; *ay:* says;
                       eo: jeopardy; *ae:* aesthetic

/i/   *i:* it; *u:* busy; *ui:* build; *y:* rhythm;
                       ie: fierce; *ee:* been; *ea:* year

/o/ or /a/ \ä\   *o:* pot; *a:* what; *e:* sergeant; *ea:* heath

/u/ or /ə/ \ə\   *u:* but; *o:* son; *ou:* cousin; *oe:* does;
                       oo: blood

/ā/ or /ey/ \ā\   *a:* bake; *ai:* wait; *ay:* may; *ea:* break;
                       ei: weigh; *ey:* obey; *au:* gauge; *et:* bouquet

/ē/ or /iy/ \ē\   *e:* me; *ee:* deed; *ea:* meat; *ei:* receive;
                       ie: believe; *ae:* caesarian; *ey:* key;
                       oe: Phoenix; *eo:* people; *i:* ravine;
                       ay: quay; *y:* soliloquy

/ī/ or /ay/ \ī\   *i:* mile; *ie:* die; *ei:* stein; *y:* try; *ai:* aisle;
                       ay: kayak; *ye:* bye; *igh:* sigh; *eye:* eye;
                       uy: buy

The Relationships of Sound

phonemic symbols	graphemes with examples
/ō/ or /o/ \ō\	*o:* bone; *oa:* boat; *ou:* boulder; *oa:* shoal; *oe:* hoe; *oo:* brooch; *ow:* slow; *ew:* sew; *eau:* beau
/ū/ or /uw/ \ü\	*u:* rule; *ue:* blue; *ui:* juice; *o:* lose; *oo:* pool; *ou:* soup; *eu:* neurotic; *oe:* shoe; *ioux:* Sioux; *ew:* few
/oo/ or /u/ \u̇\	*oo:* book; *o:* woman; *u:* pull; *ou:* would
/ou/ or /aw/ \au̇\	*ou:* mouse; *ow:* cow
/oi/ or /ɔy/ \ȯi\	*oi:* oil; *oy:* boy
/ɔu/ or /ɔ/ \ȯ\	*au:* haul; *a:* ball; *aw:* flaw; *augh:* caught; *ou:* fought; *o:* long; *oa:* broad

The following two vowel sounds occur only before the consonant "r".

/eh/ (no dictionary symbol)	*a:* care; *ai:* hair; *ea:* wear; *e:* ere; *ay:* mayor; *ei:* heir
/ə-r/ or /əh/ \ə-r\	*e:* germ; *ea:* learn; *u:* burn; *o:* worm; *ou:* courtesy; *y:* myrtle

The following sound occurs only in syllables with weak stress.

/ə/ or /ɨ/ \ə\	*a:* alone; *e:* thicken; *i:* robin; *o:* cotton; *u:* wakeup; *ai:* mountain; *eo:* surgeon; *ou:* curious; *ia:* parliament; *oi:* tortoise

Structural Characteristics as Aids to Spelling and Pronunciation

Although English is a difficult language to master, through studying the phonemic system we discover that there is some logic in its word formation and that there are certain relationships between its sound and its spelling and pronunciation. There are also certain characteristics in the structural patterns of words, as was discussed in the preceding chapter on "The Forms of Words." An awareness of these characteristics can be a great aid to both spelling and pronunciation. For example, the knowledge that words are made up of syllables, small units of sound built around a single vowel sound, is fundamental to the correct spelling and pronunciation of a word; a knowledge of word roots and affixes helps us not only to identify the meanings and functions of its syllables, but also to identify the meaning and function of the word as a whole.

Assimilation, the process by which the sounds of affixes are adapted to the sounds of the word roots they are attached to, was discussed on page 115. Many of these changes follow regular patterns that can help us in spelling and pronunciation. In some cases, the spellings of word roots are adapted when affixes are added. These changes also follow identifiable patterns.

For example, one-syllable words ending in one consonant preceded by one vowel double the final consonant before adding a suffix that begins with a vowel (such as *-ed, -en, -ing*).

fat	fatter	big	biggest
clip	clipped	sit	sitting
cut	cutter	pin	pinning

This is also true of words of more than one syllable if the accent falls on the final syllable.

contrόl	contrόlled	admίt	admίtting
forgét	forgétting	remίt	remίttance
travél	travéller	transfér	transférring

In the new word, formed by adding the suffix, the same syllable is accented.

Words ending in a silent "e" usually drop the "e" before adding a suffix beginning with a vowel.

believe	believing	arrive	arrival
imagine	imaginary	serve	servant
tense	tension	type	typist

However, the "e" is usually retained before a suffix beginning with a consonant.

state	statement	positive	positively
time	timeless	like	likeness

Among the exceptions to this pattern are "awful," "argument," "judgment," "truly," and "wholly."

When the final silent "e" is preceded by "c" or "g," the "e" is usually retained before a suffix beginning with "a" or "o." Thus "notice" becomes "noticeable." The "e" is retained in these cases because of pronunciation: we pronounce "c" with the sound of "k" when it comes before "a," and therefore we should have to pronounce "noticeable" "notikable" if we were to spell it "noticable." Other examples of this:

peace	peaceable
change	changeable
courage	courageous

Words ending in "y" preceded by a consonant change the "y" to "i" before any suffix except one beginning with "i."

lazy	lazily	deny	denial
carry	carried	marry	marriage
busy	business	plenty	plentiful
merry	merriment	study	studies

The "y" is retained when the suffix begins with "i."

study	studying	carry	carrying
baby	babyish	forty	fortyish

If the "y" is preceded by a vowel, the "y" remains unchanged when a suffix is added.

stay	stayed	monkey	monkeys
play	playful	employ	employment
delay	delays	journey	journeying

Among the exceptions to this are "lay–laid" and "say–said."

Except for those root words ending in "y" and silent "e," the spellings of most root words are not changed when suffixes or prefixes are added. For example,

thought + ful = thoughtful	thin + ness = thinness
accept + ance = acceptance	gradual + ly = gradually
mis + spell = misspell	dis + qualify = disqualify
un + equal = unequal	im + mobilize = immobilize

The spelling of the word roots or base words themselves is, of course, the most difficult problem. However, observation of the relationships of sound to meaning, spelling, and pronunciation does reveal certain patterns that can be helpful.

For example, words containing the compound graphemes "ie" and "ei" are perhaps the most difficult to spell because they vary so much. However, one helpful (but by no means infallible) observation is that when the compound grapheme represents a long "e" sound /ē/ the word is spelled "i" before "e" except after "c."

achieve	hygiene	shield
priest	thief	chief
brief	piece	siege
reprieve	niece	believe
receive	ceiling	deceit
perceive	receipt	conceit

The exceptions to this pattern are words pronounced with a long "a" /ā/.

beige	deign	eight
heinous	neigh	neighbor
feign	feint	freight
reign	rein	veil
vein	weight	weigh

Exceptions that do not fall into either pattern include "either," "neither," "financier," "foreign," "forfeit," "height," "heifer," "leisure," "seize," "weird," and "heir."

Some words have particular characteristics because of a historical event or process, or because they were borrowed from another language. An awareness of the history of the English language is invaluable to correct word usage, spelling, and pronunciation. It would take too much space, in a book of this size, to trace the development of the structural characteristics of particular words. However, there are several good books on the historical development of language, among them Margaret Schlauch's *The Gift of Tongues* (New York: The Viking Press, Inc., 1942), Mario Pei's *The Story of Language* (revised edition; Philadelphia: J. B. Lippincott Co., 1965), and Frederick Bodmer's *The Loom of Language* (New York: W. W. Norton & Company, Inc., 1944).

For example, historical development explains why some words have "silent" letters:

silent *b:*	debt, comb
silent *g:*	gnome, reign
silent *gh:*	ghost, furlough
silent *k:*	know, knight
silent *n:*	column, Lynn
silent *p:*	psychology, receipt
silent *t:*	mortgage
silent *w:*	wreath, write

History also explains why spellings that appear to be idiosyncracies in our language are in fact quite logical. For example, it explains why the spelling of the personal pronoun "they" changes to "their" and "them," and why such words as "queue" and "cue" and "their" and "there" are spelled differently.

The last examples, "queue" and "cue" and "their" and "there," are called *homonyms*, two or more words that are spelled differently and have different meanings but are pronounced in the same way. Homonyms pose one of the greatest problems in spelling. The best way to identify them is to visualize them in phrases that give clues to their meaning. The following sentences contain some examples of homonyms.

Are you **all ready**? Your guests have **already** arrived.
We had a short **break** for coffee. He **braked** abruptly to stop the car.
The **complement** is part of the predicate. He **complimented** her on her new hair style.
The dog had **coarse** hair and its owner had **coarse** manners. He drove off the **course**.
We had ice cream for **dessert**. The soldiers **deserted** their post.
The plane has **dual** controls. The men fought a **duel** in the play.
She was **affected** by the mood of the music. The new method was **effected** with a minimum of difficulty.
The decision was not **fair**. How much is the plane **fare**?
The cavalry went **forth** with courage. He came in **fourth** in the race.
Did you **hear** what I said? Come **here** at once.
The prince is **heir** to the throne. The bird flew through the **air**.
The men remained **idle** all day. The natives worshipped many **idols**.
I dropped the **key** to my front door. The boat is docked at the **quay**.

My feet are as heavy as **lead**. The girl **led** the blind lady.
A **metal** bowl is harder to clean than a ceramic one. The athletes were on their **mettle**.
The house was **plainly** furnished. He went by **plane**.
Have a **piece** of pie. The warriors made **peace**.
His **principles** are fine. The **principal** called a faculty meeting.
The **rain** spoiled my new dress. The king's **reign** lasted forty years.
He **threw** the ball. He went **through** the door.
I went **to** the party **too**. The **two** of us went home.
I am too **weak** to run. A **week** went by before he wrote.
I hate this rainy **weather**. I am not sure **whether** I shall go.
The meeting was a **waste** of time. He lost three inches from his **waist**.

Finally, here is a list of words that can easily be misspelled:

absence	accept	accidentally
acknowledge	across	acquaint
address	affect	all right
already	always	altogether
altar	amateur	among
analyze	angel	angle
answer	apparatus	apparent
appearance	argument	athletics
beginning	belief	believe
benefited	breath	breathe
business	calendar	capital
capitol	captain	cemetery
character	choose	chose
clothes	colonel	column
coming	committee	concede
conceive	conscience	conscious
consistent	corps	corpse
criticism	criticize	deceased

decision	define	definitely
definition	description	develop
different	discipline	disappear
disappointed	disastrous	disease
doesn't	effect	embarrass
emphasize	equipment	especially
excellent	except	existence
experience	familiar	fascinate
February	finally	fiery
foreign	forth	forty
fourth	friend	fulfill
fundamental	gorgeous	government
governor	grammar	handsome
height	hindrance	illusion
immediately	incidentally	inconceivable
incredible	independent	indispensable
interesting	its	it's
judgment	knew	knowledge
laid	lead	led
legitimate	library	literature
losing	loose	mathematics
meant	medicine	medieval
minute	necessary	niece
ninety	ninth	nuisance
occasion	occur	occurred
omission	omit	operate
opportunity	parallel	peculiar
particularly	permissible	personal
personnel	pleasant	practically
precede	preceding	proceeded
preferred	principal	principle
privilege	probably	professor
quiet	quite	ready
realize	really	receipt
receive	recommend	refrigerator
relevant	renaissance	resistance

respectively	restaurant	rhyme
rhythm	ridiculous	schedule
secretary	seize	separate
sergeant	similar	sincerely
sophomore	sought	stationary
stationery	suspersede	surely
surprise	suspense	temperament
their	there	they're
therefore	though	through
threw	to	too
two	tragedy	trouble
truly	Tuesday	twelfth
until	usually	villain
villein	weather	whether
whose	who's	women
writing	written	

Part Two | A New Method for Teaching the English Language

Chapter Five
The Inductive Method

The Inductive Method

Unlike the traditional method, which so often leads merely to the knowledge of a series of facts "about" the language, the New Grammar can lead to a genuine understanding of the essential nature of the English language. This understanding is achieved through what is called *the inductive method*.

The inductive method involves the learning of general concepts that can be applied to the understanding of specific facts. The more fundamental and basic the concept, the greater its breadth of applicability. The inductive method in the teaching of the New Grammar involves the observation and analysis of the basic concepts of language, such as structural patterns, word formation, and the relationships of sound to meaning, which are then applied to the understanding of such specifics as word functions, spelling, and pronunciation. The importance of the inductive method is that it encourages students to observe their language and to arrive at conclusions for themselves. It forces the students to think and to become fully involved in the learning process; the knowledge they acquire is therefore more meaningful to them and more likely to be retained.

Teaching Inductively

The most important aspect of inductive teaching is *putting the responsibility for learning upon the student*. This is difficult for many teachers, who find it easier to act as teaching "devices" rather than as "agents" of instruction. The teacher must be sure that the students are really applying the appropriate problem-solving techniques and not merely guessing possible solutions. A suitable classroom climate is essential: one that truly allows the process of self-discovery to evolve, and one in which the students are not afraid to verbalize assumptions that may be wrong. The teacher must give the students enough opportunities for validating their hypotheses and sufficient practice in applying each newly learned concept. He must be particularly tolerant, and he must be patient, encouraging, and willing to wait for answers.

The teacher must be constantly alert and well prepared. He must be ready to offer a "clue" or to ask a helpful question. He should be prepared to spend extra time designing special exercises and materials of creative value to the particular students he is teaching.

Finally, the teacher must make sure that he helps his students to look seriously at their language and to understand its basic concepts.

The Four Steps of the Inductive Method

There are four steps in the inductive method for teaching the New Grammar: (1) the identification, by the students, of the new concept; (2) the statement of the concept; (3) the testing of the new concept through the analysis of further data; and (4) the application of the new concept.

The Identification of the New Concept

The teacher gives the students examples of the concept he is introducing and helps them to identify the concept from the examples. This can be done on a class basis with the examples read aloud or written on the blackboard, or on an individual basis with written examples. The important part of this first step is that *the students identify for themselves the basic concept to be learned.* The teacher can offer "clues" to help the students derive the concept from the examples, but the final assumption must come from them. (Examples of such "clues": "In which part of the sentence does the word appear?" "What do you notice about the word order?"

"What function does the word perform in the sentence?" "Do you notice any signal words?" "What do you notice about the form of the word?")

The Statement of the New Concept
When the students have identified the new concept—and only then—the concept is verbalized. While this may be done by the teacher, it is preferably done by the students. Examples of the expression of new concepts: "the subject always precedes the predicate"; "the complement completes the sense of the verb"; "a pronoun substitutes for a noun." The new concept is more meaningful to the students when they themselves have made a statement about it.

The Testing of the New Concept
When the new concept has been clearly established, the students should have further experience in identifying it—that is, they should have an opportunity to test it by analyzing further examples. To make sure that every child in the class clearly understands the lesson, exercises should be assigned and completed individually. The more imaginative teacher may use puzzles or games, or various examples from literature. It is suggested that each teacher develop his own examples, suiting them to the level and interests of his students. The most important thing about assignments to test comprehension is that they should absorb the students—they should be interesting and fun to do. They should be challenging, but at the same time they should be within the children's capabilities.

The Application of the New Concept
Experience in identifying a concept is not enough to test real comprehension. The students must apply their new knowledge by making up their own sentences. The teacher can devise a variety of ways to stimulate the students to apply new concepts to sentence construction. The simplest method is to ask them to write a series of unrelated sentences incorporating the new concept; once

they can do this, however, it is a good idea to ask them to write a series of sentences that can be connected into a story or short composition. In this way the students will see immediately how the new concept can be applied to writing. Sometimes the teacher can assign a topic for the story (by actually giving them the title or by showing them a picture and asking them to write about it), but at other times he should let the children choose their own topics.

In the teaching outline presented in the next section of this chapter, the four steps of the inductive method are demonstrated in the introduction of the first basic concepts of the New Grammar, enabling the teacher to see how they are applied. (The secondary concepts that follow are not discussed in such detail, as this information is included in Part I of this book.)

In *the sequential approach* to teaching the New Grammar, presented in the teaching outline, each concept is dealt with one by one, the teacher making sure that each is fully understood before introducing the next. This approach is therefore most suitable for elementary students, or students who have not been exposed to other methods of grammar teaching.

The "Janglish" approach, presented in the second section of this chapter, is more suitable for older students who already have some understanding of the English language. It is also particularly useful in reviewing concepts learned earlier by the sequential approach and is an effective way of introducing the New Grammar to students who have been brought up on traditional grammar. Unlike the sequential method, it deals with all of the basic structural characteristics of the English language in one or two lessons and then goes back to deal with each one more specifically. It helps the students to understand language structurally, semantically, and in terms of its basic concepts rather than as a series of rules and definitions.

The Sequential Approach

Many decisions concerning the order in which to teach the concepts of the New Grammar must ultimately be made by the teacher because only he can judge the readiness of his students.

Spelling, punctuation, and the history of language, for example, may be introduced whenever the teacher feels that they are appropriate and that his students can deal with them effectively. There is, however, a certain logical sequence that should be followed in teaching the New Grammar. While changes may be made in the sequence of presentation of some of the secondary concepts (such as the prepositional phrase), the primary concepts (such as the basic sentence patterns) must be taught in a definite order. The suggested outline that follows should therefore serve the teacher as a guide in deciding the appropriate sequence for teaching the primary concepts of the New Grammar.

Teaching the Essential Elements of the Kernel Sentences

In contrast to traditional grammar, which begins with the identification of isolated words—"the noun," "the verb," "the adjective"—the New Grammar begins with *the sentence.*

We begin with the sentence for several reasons. First, it is our basic means of communication and forms the core or kernel of our language. Secondly, it makes the students think in terms of general concepts from the very beginning. These concepts, such as word order, the relationship of one word to another, and the function of words in regard to meaning, can be applied to the understanding of the most complex structures later on. Finally, children come to school with an initial grasp of the basic patterns of our language and are therefore capable of handling simple sentence analysis.

Although children use quite complex patterns in daily conversation, we begin teaching grammar through analysis of the very simplest kernel sentences. This enables the students to identify the essential elements quickly and easily without distractions. Also, because the sentences are well within their grasp, the students make few mistakes and are encouraged by their success—always an important factor in the learning process.

The first and most important concept to teach is the subject-predicate structure of the sentence. This is done through the analysis of simple two-word, noun-verb sentences.

The Verb

The students first learn to identify the verb because it is the most important part of the sentence. One of the best ways to begin the identification of the verb is to ask the students what they do each day and to list their responses on the blackboard. For example: "I get up." "I eat." "I walk." "I look." Sometimes the students offer more complex sentences—for example: "I eat breakfast." "I drink milk." "I walk to school." The teacher should ignore these complements at this stage.

As the lesson continues the students will notice that while most of the words they offer are accepted, some are not. For example, they may notice that while "sing," "run," and "play" are accepted, such words as "song," "runner," and "player" are not. The words that are accepted they learn are *verbs,* and they learn that a verb is part of the *predicate.*

Developing the students' ability to recognize verbs is the most important aspect of New Grammar teaching. Once this skill is mastered, the identification of the subject and predicate—the other two essential elements of the sentence—becomes largely a matter of common sense. The concept of the verb is one of the most difficult to teach, particularly in its more complex forms. But if the teacher begins with examples and exposes his students to a wide number of these examples, he will provide a good foundation upon which to build the more difficult concepts of predication later. Remember that in the New Grammar one concept is built upon another and thus, if the teacher has done his groundwork well, the students will progress with comparative ease.

Identifying the verb. The teacher now reverses the earlier process by giving the students sentences and asking them to identify the verb in each. The sentences may be given verbally, but preferably they are written on the blackboard in a second column beside the students' sentences. In these sentences, subjects different from the "I" offered by the students should be used: "Miss Brown teaches," "Miss Brown laughs," "dogs bark," "babies cry," "men talk," "John came," and so on. As yet, no reference to these subjects should be made; they are introduced in this way only to develop a general awareness of the next concept to be taught.

The students usually identify the verbs easily. When they have done this, the teacher poses the question, "How did you know they were verbs?" The answer most often comes quickly, but if the students do have difficulty, a second question can be asked: "Where does the verb come in the sentence?" This will bring the reply, "It comes second," or "It comes last." Once the students have discovered for themselves this first and most basic concept of sentence structure, the teacher may verbalize the concept.

Stating the verb concept. "The verb, which is part of the predicate, comes in the last part of the sentence." At the same time the teacher makes this statement, he gives the students another way to identify verbs: "If the word fits into the framework, 'They might _____(them),' it is a verb."

Testing the verb concept. Once the concept of the verb is clearly established, the students must practice identifying verbs on their own. One method is to assign exercises consisting of simple verb-noun sentences in which the student is asked either to underline or to circle the verbs. Another method, which is particularly enjoyed by younger students, is to give them two words, each on a separate 3 x 5-inch card, and ask them to put the cards in the correct sentence order.

Applying the verb concept. When the teacher is sure that each child can identify verbs without difficulty, the students are asked to make up their own sentences, putting the verbs in the proper positions. The teacher must remember to limit the sentences to two words or else the students will produce quite complicated structures and will quickly become confused. If the students are bright and capable, they can construct short "stories" using simple noun-verb patterns. For example: "John came. John ate. He drank. He left."

The teacher may be surprised to find that the students are including in these sentences such complicated grammatical elements as pronouns, plurals, and different tenses. In fact, this is to be expected because these elements occur automatically in the students' daily conversation. At this stage, however, the students are not really aware of the complexity of these elements and should not be made aware of it until the basic essentials of sentence structure are fully understood. The teacher should accept the variations, but at this stage should make no reference to them.

The Subject

Identifying the subject. Having learned to identify the verb, the students next learn to identify the subject. Referring to the list of two-word sentences already on the blackboard, the teacher draws the students' attention to their subjects and asks, "What do you notice about these words?" The response usually comes rapidly, "They come before the verb," or "They come first in the sentence."

Having established this second important concept, the teacher draws the students' attention to the different subjects of some of the sentences—for example, "I walk," "Miss Brown teaches," "dogs bark," "babies cry." He then asks, "What do these words do?" When the answer—"They tell more about the verb"—is given, the teacher asks for possible substitutions for the subject "I" in the first column of sentences, those originally offered by the students. The "I's" are erased and the new words are written in their places. Again the students discover that while most of their words are accepted, some are not. The reason for this, the teacher reminds them, is that these words do not tell more about the verb.

Stating the subject concept. "A *subject* always comes first in a sentence and it tells us more about the verb. It answers the questions 'who?' or 'what?'" The second statement may be illustrated by examples:

Joan walks.	Who walks?	Joan
The tree fell.	What fell?	the tree

At this time, the teacher tells the students that the words used as subjects are called *nouns*. He also gives them a framework for identifying nouns: "I was thinking of _____ (s)."

Testing the subject concept. The same types of exercises and games that were used to test the identification of verbs may be used in this lesson. However, the teacher will find that, if he taught the first lesson on verbs well, fewer examples will be needed because the students will recognize subjects fairly quickly and easily.

Applying the subject concept. The students may now construct their own sentences (orally and in written form) and make up stories. Again, these sentences should be limited to simple noun-verb constructions. It is also a good idea to assign exercises asking for substitutions for the subjects and/or verbs before going on to the final essential element of the sentence, the complement.

The Complement

Identifying the complement. The teacher begins the identification of the complement by referring only to the direct object, that is, by using the simple noun-verb-noun sentence pattern. As examples of this pattern, he may use those sentences suggested by the students when verbs were first listed on the blackboard that contained direct objects: "I eat breakfast," "I drink milk," and so on.

The teacher asks, "How do these sentences differ from those that are already on the blackboard? What is the difference between 'I eat breakfast' and 'I eat'?" The students should be able to arrive at the answer, "Both have a subject and a verb, but the first sentence contains something else."

The teacher's next question is, "What does this something else do?" The students usually find the answer to this simple: "It tells us more about the verb." If they do not find the answer immediately, they soon will if they are given more sentences to work with. For example, "What do the words 'cornflakes,' 'dinner,' and 'apples' do in the following sentences?"

    I eat cornflakes.   I eat dinner.   I eat apples.

"What do the words 'mouse,' 'books,' and 'boat' do in the following sentences?"

The cat chased the mouse.   I read books.   He sails a boat.

Once the students have grasped the initial idea of the complement, the teacher asks them to suggest the kinds of questions they might ask themselves to identify a complement. They discover that these are the very same questions that helped them to identify the subject: "The complement answers the questions 'who?' ('whom?') or 'what?' "

The cat chased the mouse.	The cat chased whom?	the mouse
I read books.	I read what?	books
He sails a boat.	He sails what?	a boat

This discovery leads them to the generalization that nouns can be used after verbs as well as before verbs. They now learn that while a noun is called the subject when it comes before the verb, it is called the (direct) *object* when it comes after the verb. (The teacher should not include the word "direct" until he teaches the difference between direct and indirect objects.) They also learn that the object is part of the *complement*.

Stating the complement concept. At this point, the teacher may put all of these new discoveries into a clear and comprehensive statement, or he may ask the students to make such a statement: "The complement of a sentence comes after the verb and tells us more about the verb; it completes the sense of the verb. It can be called an object, and it is a noun because it answers the questions 'who?' 'whom?' or 'what?' and fits into the framework, 'I was thinking of _____ (s).' "

Testing the complement concept. The students should be given sentences that contain subjects, verbs, and direct objects and asked to identify the verbs first. They should be reminded at this stage that the verb is the most important part of the sentence and that once they can identify the verb, the other parts will be easy to find. When they have identified the verbs, they should next find the subjects and then the objects. As in the earlier lessons, the teacher should try to develop exercises that will hold the children's interest.

Applying the complement concept. The students may now develop their own sentences and stories using the noun-verb-noun sentence pattern. This step may be combined with the preceding one; that is, the sentences made up by one student may be used by another as an exercise for testing identification of the words. For example, partners may exchange sentences, identify the words, and then compare answers. This is an effective way to teach—the students enjoy it, and the discussion among themselves of their answers reinforces the learning process.

The students have now learned the first two basic sentence patterns, the noun-verb and the noun-verb-noun. They realize that a sentence can consist of a subject and verb only, but that it sometimes needs a complement to complete its meaning.

Expanding the Essential Elements of the Kernel Sentences

Now that they are familiar with the first two basic sentence patterns, the students should be introduced to the terms *noun phrase* and *verb phrase*—this not only draws together the concepts they have just learned, it also leads to the identification and use of signal words and, later, modifying words.

Through the usual questioning method, the teacher helps the students to see that "a subject consists of a noun phrase, which can be made up of a single noun or a group of words 'clustered' around the noun," and that "a predicate consists of a verb phrase, which can be made up of a single verb or a verb followed by a group of words that completes its sense, the complement." The noun, they learn, is called the "headword" of the subject, while the verb is the "headword" of the predicate.

The teacher gives the students expanded sentences (still in the noun-verb and noun-verb-noun patterns) and asks them to identify the headwords.

Determiners

Now that the sentences contain more varied words, the teacher draws the students' attention to the fact that nouns usually name people or things and that they are usually preceded by a certain kind of word. Using the four steps of the inductive method, the teacher leads them to see that "determiners, such as 'the,' 'a,' 'some,' 'this,' and 'that,' usually precede a noun and therefore can be used as signals to identify nouns. These determiners also tell, or determine, the meaning of a noun. For example, 'the' boy means some particular boy, while 'a' boy means any boy."

Personal Pronouns

The concept of determiners leads easily to that of possessive personal pronouns, which, when used as noun modifiers indicating possession, function much like determiners. For example, "my" dog means the dog that belongs to me and not to anyone else, "your" dog means the dog that belongs to you, "their" dog means the dog that belongs to them, and so on.

It is often a good idea to introduce next the fact that some nouns are written with capital letters ("Miss Brown," "Los Angeles," "Joan") and that certain words can *substitute* for nouns. Personal pronouns should be dealt with first ("I," "you," "he," "we," "they"), then indefinite pronouns ("anyone," "someone," "nobody," "nothing"), and then possessive personal pronouns used as noun substitutes ("mine," "yours," "his," "ours," "theirs"). The use of determiners as noun substitutes may also be presented.

The Noun-Linking Verb-Noun Sentence Pattern

Now that the students have a better understanding of the noun phrase, they should be introduced to some of the more intricate parts of the verb phrase, beginning with the identification of the linking verb. The teacher gives the students a set of sentences containing the verb "to be" and asks them to identify first the subject and then the verb. For example,

> I am a boy.
> You are a girl.
> Joan is my sister.
> We are students.
> You are students.
> The books are mine.

The teacher asks the students if they notice a similarity in the verbs and, when the similarity is correctly pointed out, he explains that the forms of the verb "to be" are

> I am, you are, he (she, it) is, we are, you are, they are;
> I was, you were, he (she, it) was, we were, you were, they were.

He helps the students to observe that forms of the verb "to be" must have other words after them (complements) and that these words are often noun phrases. This introduces the students to the third basic sentence pattern, the noun-linking verb-noun pattern. They learn that the verb is called a *linking verb* because it "links" the complement (which tells more about the subject) to the subject.

The students should be given plenty of opportunity to practice identifying linking verbs and their noun-phrase complements before the fourth sentence pattern, noun-linking verb-adjective, is introduced. When they can handle the verb "to be" with ease, they should also become familiar with some of the other linking verbs, such as "seem," "look," "appear," "taste," "smell," and "become."

The terms "transitive" and "intransitive" may also be introduced at this point, although it is not necessary. Remember that too many terms can be confusing—the important thing is that the students understand and apply the *concepts*.

The Noun-Linking Verb-Adjective Pattern

At this point, the teacher may prefer to introduce the adjective first as the noun modifier in a noun phrase—"the pretty girl came." However, many teachers have found that an understanding of the noun-linking verb-adjective structure—"the girl is pretty"—brings with it an understanding of the function of the adjective.

The students will enjoy learning about and using the adjective because it helps them to communicate more expressively. But the teacher should remind them that the noun and the verb are the most important and expressive words in our language, and that *modifiers* (of which the adjective is one form) are only used to *supplement* these words. If this point of view can be established early in language learning, many future problems in writing will be prevented.

The students should have plenty of experience in working with the third and fourth sentence patterns so that they will acquire a real understanding of the difference between them. For example, they can be asked to substitute words for the predicate noun and then for the predicate adjective.

> Joan is a girl. (a classmate) (an athlete) (my sister)
> Joan is pretty. (sad) (tall) (smart) (angry) (happy)

The teacher must constantly revise with the students the concepts they have learned previously. The time for revision will depend on the students—the questions they ask, the difficulties they encounter, and the readiness they show to accept refinements in the basic concepts. The presentation of the modifying function of the adjective and of its placement *before* the noun and *after* the linking verb offers an opportunity to review and refine somewhat the concept of word order and to stress its importance in our language.

Plurals
Now that the students have a good grasp of the first four basic sentence patterns, it is advisable to begin to look at some of the characteristic structures of words. In fact, these can be introduced much earlier, as early as the first noun-verb sentence pattern.

Again, it is for the teacher to decide when his students are most ready for each new concept.

The students will have met the plural form already in many of the sentences they have had to deal with, but they are now led to observe how plurals function and how they are formed. As in much of New Grammar teaching, it is a case of making the students aware of concepts they are already using.

The plural forms of nouns should be dealt with first, these being easier than the concept of the verb plural. The plural forms of the various types of pronouns should be introduced next, first the personal pronouns ("I–we," "you–you," "he, she, it–they"), possessive pronouns ("mine–ours," "yours–yours," "his, hers, its–theirs"), and indefinite pronouns used as noun substitutes, and then the possessive pronouns used as noun modifiers ("my– our," "your–your," "his, her, its–their"). The determiners that change form to indicate the plural may also be introduced here.

The students learn that the noun-modifying word, the adjective, does not change to indicate the plural.

The verb plural is now taught, the students learning that verbs change to indicate number only in the *third person singular* (when the subject is "he," "she," "it," "Juan," "the teacher," and so on) and only in the *present tense*. (If the students ask about it, the teacher may wish to review the forms of the verb "to be" with them and to explain that it is the only exception to this pattern.)

The Verb Tenses

Discussion of the verb plural leads directly to an analysis of verb tenses. Again, teaching the verb tenses is largely a matter of making the students aware of structures that they already use automatically. At this stage they should become familiar with the infinitive form and the past form of the regular verb. When they have grasped these, the present participle may be introduced. They should also become familiar with the tenses of the verb "to have" and with the other tenses of the verb "to be," these irregular verbs being so important in the formation of sentences. The other irregular verbs can be introduced over a period of time at the teacher's discretion.

The Auxiliary Verbs
Through the usual method of examples and questions, the discussion of the forms of the irregular verbs "to be" and "to have" can be directed toward the introduction of these verbs as auxiliary or "helping" verbs, and their combinations with the present participle and with the past form to make up the past participle can be explained.

Suffixes
The concept of verb tense forms provides an introduction to the use of suffixes. The teacher should explain the basic formation of words and the important concept of *morphemes*. Some teachers prefer to introduce this concept much earlier, often with the introduction of the plural; other teachers, however, feel that it is more appropriate at this stage. If it is taught now, the teacher should refer back to the plural lesson, asking the students when they have previously added a morpheme to change the meaning of a word.

The Possessive Case
Having observed how morphemes may be used to change the meanings of words to form verb tenses and plurals, the students now see how they are used to change the meanings of nouns (and indefinite pronouns) to indicate possession. They learn that the verb showing possession is "to have," whose forms they know already. For example, "John has a ball."

Next, they learn that possession may also be expressed by the addition of an apostrophe and the morpheme *s* to a singular noun (or an apostrophe only to a plural noun) and by a change in the word order of the basic sentence pattern.

       John has a ball.   The boys have a ball.
       John's ball   the boys' ball

The students observe that while the first two examples are the noun-verb-noun sentence pattern with which they are familiar, the second two are not complete sentence patterns but noun phrases. The object of the sentences, "ball," has become the headword of the noun phrases; the verbs "has" and "have" and the determiner "a" have been replaced by the morpheme *s* and/or the apostrophe that was added to the original subjects of the sentences. "The boys" and "John " have thus become possessive modifiers of the headword "ball."

The students learn that possession may also be expressed by changing the word order and adding the word "of."

```
John has a ball.          The boys have a ball.
John's ball               the boys' ball
the ball of John          the ball of the boys
```

The Negative Sentence
The introduction of the negative sentence can vary, although it is best to teach it after the students have become familiar with auxiliary verbs. The negative sentence is presented as a simple *transformation* of the basic sentence patterns.

The Adverb
It is now time to introduce the last word class, adverbs. In teaching the word classes, remember that the students must understand the words of each class in terms of their functions and must recognize them in terms of their structure, position in the sentence, and characteristic signal words. Remember also that adverbs are the most difficult word class to identify because they function in a variety of ways and are often similar in form to the other word classes.

Single-word adverbs, such as "happily," "quickly," and "slowly," should be introduced first, and the students' attention should be drawn to their characteristic suffix, *-ly*.

Noun Phrases, Adjectives, and Adverbs in the Predicate Position
In order to help the students identify the differences between

predicate noun phrases, adjectives, and adverbs, it is a good idea to review and revise the concepts of the predicate noun phrase and the predicate adjective at this point. It cannot be overemphasized how necessary it is for the students to have adequate experience in identifying the different functions of these three predicates.

The teacher should now go into more detail concerning the different forms and functions of the word classes. The students become aware of such things as the comparative forms of adjectives and adverbs and their correct usage. For example, they learn why we cannot say "it looked real nice" and "I feel badly" but must say "it really looked nice" and "I felt bad." A useful and entertaining way to help the students understand the forms and functions of the word classes is to have them change words from one class to another by the use of morphemes. This exercise can also be done with verbs.

The Fifth Kernel Sentence Pattern
Many teachers find that it is appropriate to introduce Pattern 5 in its three variations at this stage. Although this pattern is the most complex, all of its elements except the indirect object should now be familiar to the students.

When Pattern 5 has been mastered, it is a good idea to have a general revision of all the basic sentence patterns and all the transformations (both by rearrangement of the basic elements and by introduction of new elements into the basic patterns) that have been taught up to this point. The areas where the students seem to be weak should obviously be revised in detail.

The Question
Now that the students are familiar with the five kernel sentence patterns, they should learn how to transform them into questions. This concept, however, may be introduced much earlier.

The Prepositional Phrase
When the students can handle the five kernel sentence patterns and their simple transformations with ease, they learn how the

patterns can be expanded. They have already had some practice at this (for example, with the introduction of the single-word modifiers), but they now learn how sentences are expanded through the introduction of word-groups—phrases and clauses.

The first word-group to be presented is usually the prepositional phrase, although some teachers prefer to present it much earlier than this, even as early as the linking verb. Again, this must be left to the discretion of the teacher. If the prepositional phrase is taught at this point, the teacher should remind the students that they have met it once before, when studying the formation of the possessive case ("the ball of John").

The Verb Functions
Now that the sentences are becoming more complicated, with more words and structures added to them, the students should become acquainted with the other tenses and functions of the verb. At this stage, the teacher can also draw attention to the verbs that are often used incorrectly, such as "lie—lay" and "rise—raise."

Continued Expansion of the Kernel Sentences
The students are gradually introduced—as always, through the four steps of the inductive method—to the more complex forms of sentence expansion.

By this time the students should have a thorough knowledge of the fundamentals of their language. From now on they should learn how to use these fundamentals in more sophisticated forms of written and oral communication. However, the teacher is reminded that it is wise to revise the basic concepts constantly—but always in new and interesting ways so that the students will not become bored. Finally, the teacher is reminded that his task is to help the students to enjoy manipulating their language for the clear and comprehensive expression of their ideas.

The "Janglish" Approach

The "Janglish" approach to teaching the New Grammar is

the use of nonsense words to explain the relationship of structure and meaning in our language. The idea was first developed by Fries, but has been used in a variety of ways since. The advantage of "Janglish" is that it can illustrate the basic concepts of English without any of its irregularities or complexities. A secondary advantage, but an important one, is that students enjoy it greatly, and it is thus a very stimulating teaching device.

As was mentioned earlier, the "Janglish" approach presents all of the basic characteristics of the structure of the English language in one or two lessons and then goes back to deal with each more specifically; it is therefore most appropriate for older students who already have some understanding of English. "Janglish" is, however, also an effective way to introduce the New Grammar to students who have been brought up on traditional grammar as it helps them to see language structurally rather than as a series of definitions. "Janglish" is also an excellent means for reviewing and revising the concepts already learned by the sequential approach.

The "Janglish" approach focuses attention upon the following concepts, usually in this order: (1) the importance of word order in the sentence, (2) the functions of words within the sentence, (3) the ways to identify the word classes, and (4) the kernel sentences and the ways in which they may be transformed. As in all approaches to the New Grammar, the main focus is upon the sentence, our basic means of communication, and the method of teaching is inductive.

The Importance of Word Order in the Sentence

The students are introduced to the essential elements of the sentence and their basic order through sentences consisting of "Janglish" words (which are used only in place of the four word classes) and function words. The words of these sentences, however, are arranged in unusual order.

The words may be written on the blackboard, although a magnetic board on which they can be rearranged easily is more effective. Another good method is to use cards, one for each word, which can either be held and rearranged by students in front of the class, or rearranged by the students on their own.

> jangents on the janged jangor janger a the

Having presented this nonsense sentence, the teacher asks the students to rearrange the words into a sensible order. They usually do this surprisingly quickly, presenting such rearrangements as:

> the jangents on the janger janged a jangor;
> a jangor janged the jangents on the janger;
> the janger on a jangor janged the jangents;
> on the jangor a janger janged the jangents.

After they have produced these sentence patterns, the students are asked to substitute English words for the "Janglish" words. In this way, they relate the concept of word order specifically to their own familiar language.

The Functions of Words Within the Sentence

Having helped the students to identify the importance of word order in our language, the teacher turns their attention to the ways words function within a sentence.

First, he asks the students if they can make any sense out of the "Janglish" sentences. Can they, for example, extract any meaning from the following sentence?

> The jangents on the janger janged a jangor.

The students usually respond with observations like the following:

> The jangents did something to a jangor;
> A jangor is the thing that was janged;
> The event took place on the janger.

These observations lead to the realization that different words perform different functions. For example, words like "janged" *do* something; words like "jangor" and "jangent" are *things* that do something or have something done to them; and words like "on" indicate *where* something happened.

Through the usual questioning method, the teacher helps the students to clarify and restate these observations. For example:

1. The chief function of the verb is predication—in this case, it tells us what the "jangents" did to the "jangor."
2. A noun can function as a subject, an object, and an object of a preposition in a sentence.

subject	object of a preposition		direct object
The jangents	on the janger	janged	a jangor

3. Words can function to tell us more about other words—in this case, the words "on the janger" tell us more about "the jangents."

At this point, the teacher can progress to new "Janglish" sentences containing substitutes for adjectives, adverbs, and pronouns in order to explain their functions, or he can leave these until later and continue on to the identification of the word classes.

The Ways to Identify the Word Classes

The Structural Characteristics of Words
The teacher first draws the students' attention to the words that are easiest to identify in the sentence, the nouns ("jangents," "janger," "jangor"). He asks, "What do you notice about the structure of these words, particularly their endings?"

The students' answers lead to the identification of the noun suffixes *-ents, -er,* and *-or.* They are next asked to suggest other endings that could be exchanged for these without changing the words' function as nouns. This leads to the identification of such suffixes as *-ist, -ess, -ship,* and *-dom.* The teacher points out the function of morphemes and explains the difference between derivational morphemes (such as *-ness, -ity, -tion, -ment, -ship,* and

-dom) and inflectional morphemes (such as *-s* and *-'s*).

The teacher can ask the students to identify the morphemes that would change the nouns into verbs, adjectives, and adverbs, thus explaining the structural characteristics of all the word classes together, or he may leave these until later and continue with the identification of the noun.

The Presence of Signal Words

Having identified the structural characteristics of nouns (or of all the word classes), the teacher asks, "Do you notice any words that 'signal' the presence of nouns?"

> The jangents on the janger janged a jangor.

This leads the students to recognize that such words as "the" and "a" serve as signals for nouns. The students learn that these are function words called determiners, and that other determiners are such words as "some," "this," "these," and "that."

The Position of Words

At this point, the students are reminded that observing the positions of words, which they have already done in identifying the different functions of words, is another way in which to identify the word classes.

Stress in Words

Finally, the students are made aware that some words can be recognized by the differences in stress given to their parts. They are asked which parts of the words "jangents," "jangor," and "janger" they naturally stress in speaking, and which part of the word "janged." They discover that stress is put on the first part of nouns and the last part of verbs.

nouns	verbs
jángents	jangéd
récord	recórd

address address
concert concert

The Kernel Sentence Patterns and Their Transformations

Next, the teacher uses new "Janglish" sentences to introduce the five kernel sentence patterns and to show how they can be transformed into questions, and negative and passive statements.

The Kernel Sentences

Pattern 1:

noun	verb
The jangist	jangs.

Pattern 2:

noun	verb	noun
A jangess	janged	that jangdom.

Pattern 3:

noun	linking verb	noun
These jangents	are	jangers.

Pattern 4:

noun	linking verb	adjective
Jangents	are	jangary.

Pattern 5:

noun	verb	noun	noun
Her jangor	is janging	the jangents	a jangship.
The jangers	janged	their jangor	jangent.

noun	verb	noun	adjective
The janger	jangs	his jangors	janable.

The Inverted Question Patterns
With the verbs "to be" and "to have":

	predicate	subject	complement
	Have	the jangors	a jangent?
	Are	these jangists	janary?

With the addition of an auxiliary verb:

auxiliary	subject	predicate	complement
Do	you	jan	the jangors?
Did	they	jan	these jangists?

With the addition of "wh" words:

"wh" word	auxiliary	subject	predicate	complement
When	are	these jangents	janning?	
Where	has	the jangor	janned?	
How	will	you	jang	this janger?

The Negative Pattern

subject	auxiliary	negative	predicate	complement
My jangist	is	not	janging	the jangents.
Her jangship	has	not	janged jangly.	

The Passive Pattern

subject	auxiliary	verb "to be"	predicate	"by" prepositional phrase
The jangor	has	been	janged	by the jangent.

The teacher can find countless ways in which to use "Janglish" to explain the basic concepts of the English language—the approach is simple and is thoroughly enjoyed by students. However, it is more successful when used with students who already have some understanding of the fundamentals of the language.

Chapter Six
The Relationships of Grammar to Literature, Writing, and Usage

Developing Language Skills

We teach grammar so that our students may communicate more effectively. Therefore we do not teach it as an isolated subject but seek to relate it closely to the skills of reading, writing, listening, and speaking. Making these relationships meaningful to students, however, is perhaps one of the most difficult and time-consuming aspects of English teaching. The following suggestions on the selection of literary, written, and oral assignments are intended to help the teacher with this task.

Relating the New Grammar to Literature

Literature can be used very effectively in teaching the New Grammar because it provides the students with an opportunity to see how the fundamentals they are learning have been applied by others. It shows them that grammar is not a mere "science" but a working tool that can be used in a variety of ways to convey an endless number of feelings, impressions, thoughts, and ideas. It can change a grammar lesson from a mundane analysis of sentences to an experience of verbal virtuosity and syntactical ingenuity. In short, literature shows the students how grammar can, and should, be used.

There are three main ways in which selections from literature may be used in New Grammar teaching. They may be used (1) to identify a concept, (2) to compare the ways in which a concept can be applied, and (3) to provide models and frameworks for student writing and exercises.

In using a literary selection to identify a concept, for example, the teacher might ask questions like the following:

> How many sentence patterns do you notice?
> What words are functioning as subjects?
> What do you notice about the use of appositives?
> How does the author's use of subordination contribute to the effectiveness of his description?

To compare the applications of concepts, the teacher might ask questions like these:

> How does the sentence structure differ in these two passages? Why does one author sometimes use the passive voice while the other uses only the active voice? Which passage is the most effective? Why?

> Which words are used as nouns in the first passage, and which words are used as verbs in the second passage? Which passage uses more nouns than adjectives? How do these words convey a more static or a more dynamic feeling in each passage?

Using literary selections as models and frameworks for student writing and exercises, the teacher might give the following instructions:

> Notice the sentence structure in this selection and see if you can copy it using a different topic.

> Change the single-word modifiers in this passage to word-group modifiers.

> Expand the author's sentences by adding your own subordinations. How do these change the effectiveness of the sentences?

Analyze the author's use of verbals and see if you can copy his style.

In all such questions and assignments, the teacher should limit the concept to be taught—a student will gain more from an assignment if he can concentrate on one or two key aspects of the selection. The questions or instructions should be short and clear, and should apply specifically to the passage.

In choosing literary selections, the first and perhaps the most obvious principle is that the concept under consideration be easily identifiable in the selection. Some kinds of literature are clearly better than others for teaching certain concepts—descriptive writing, for instance, is best for the identification and analysis of noun clusters, adjectives, and appositives, while narrative writing is best for the analysis of verbs and kernel sentence patterns. The examples should also be good ones, illustrating the application of the concept clearly and inventively.

Secondly, the selection should contain an adequate number of examples of the concept to be identified. It should also be long enough to be comprehensible; that is, it should be an entity in itself so that the students can see the total meaning and effect toward which each sentence is contributing.

Finally, the selection should be appropriate to the level of ability and to the interests of the students. For instance, they should not be confronted with words they do not understand or they will be distracted from the main task at hand—identifying the grammatical concept.

Selections can be made from all kinds of literature, fiction and non-fiction: novels, short stories, plays, poetry, essays, magazine and newspaper articles, speeches, and so on. They need not always be written—recordings of poetry, stories, and plays are often useful, as are tapes of speeches and radio and television programs. When using oral selections, the teacher should take particular care to see that the concepts can be identified easily because they are more difficult for the students to work with than written selections. It is sometimes a good idea to take selections from the regularly assigned reading books as the students are already familiar with the passages. It is also an excellent idea to use the students' own writings—this makes the lesson particularly meaningful to them.

Literature can be a useful and stimulating aid to grammar teaching, but it must be used with care. If it is used too frequently and presented merely as a tool for grammatical analysis, the children's interest in reading may diminish rather than increase. Remember that novels, stories, and plays were not written for analysis, and that we just use them occasionally to show how effectively language can be manipulated to express our ideas and emotions. Remember too that the selections should always serve to enlarge the children's appreciation of literature as well as their understanding of grammar.

Relating the New Grammar to Writing

One of the hardest tasks for the student is to relate grammatical concepts to his writing. It is an equally hard task for the teacher to assist him in this. One of the greatest advantages of the New Grammar, however, is that it really helps to overcome this problem because it reveals how language operates rather than merely providing a series of definitions concerning the language. Not only does it illustrate the basic sentence patterns upon which English is built, it also illustrates how these patterns can be developed or transformed into all of the structures that make writing so effective and meaningful. In short, the New Grammar really can help students to write better.

In order for the New Grammar to be most helpful to the development of the students' writing skills, the teacher must make sure that they have ample opportunity to apply their grammatical knowledge to the writing situation. This means that writing assignments should be given each and every time a new concept is introduced. It does not mean, however, that all writing assignments should be specifically related to learning grammar—this would lead to the development of very stilted styles and would discourage the spontaneous, creative writing that we would like students to produce. Writing assignments must be balanced between those related to grammar learning and those aimed solely at self-expression and free invention so that the students will acquire better writing techniques and yet will remain free to develop their own styles. Writing assignments are therefore used for two main purposes: to assist students in understanding and applying grammatical concepts, and to assist them in developing their own individual styles of writing.

In grammar teaching, writing assignments are used in the fourth step of the inductive method in which students apply the concept that they have just learned. They are also used to revise concepts that were learned previously. And, although it is not assigned primarily for this purpose and is never presented to the students as a teaching tool, the students' "free" or "expressive" writing can be used as a diagnostic test—every so often the teacher should review this writing to see which concepts are not being applied and should then design specific writing assignments to revise these concepts.

In giving writing assignments, the teacher should make very clear to the students exactly which concepts they are to use in the completion of the assignment, and he should limit the number of concepts to one or two so that the students may concentrate on these. The assignment should be long enough to be challenging and to test the students' skill in applying the concept, but it should also be short enough to retain their interest. The length of each assignment will depend to some degree, however, on the concept being taught and the level of the students' ability. (Before giving the assignment, of course, the teacher should be sure that the students are fully capable of handling the concept at this particular stage in their learning.)

Literature and writing assignments should be used not only to teach specific grammatical concepts and to develop individual styles of writing but also to introduce the students to language skills and language arts in general. Thus the teacher should try to give assignments that provide experience in the following areas:

the purposes of language—to communicate information, to

to express feelings, to affect the feelings of others, and to influence the action of others;

the categories of writing—exposition, narration, description, and argumentation;

the methods of developing compositions—by the inclusion of detail, by example, by comparison or contrast, by cause and effect, and by analogy or anecdote;

the levels of usage—formal, informal, and non-standard;

the interpretation of language—tone and point of view.

Relating the New Grammar to Usage

The problem of teaching "usage," or the application of grammar to speech, has received a great deal of attention during recent years. There have been many conflicting opinions as to how it should be taught, if it should be taught, and even as to whether it can be taught. There is, in fact, controversy over the meaning of the term "usage." Is there, for example, a "correct" usage? Is there a certain "norm" of speech that we should all conform to? What about dialects? Are these correct or acceptable? Are they, perhaps, acceptable only in certain areas of the country?

As yet, these and many other questions remain unanswered. It must therefore be left to the teacher to decide how he should teach usage. His commitment is to his students and he should teach them in ways that he feels will best help *them* to communicate effectively.

However, there are certain common errors in usage that the teacher should bring to the attention of his students. Many of them are mentioned in Part I of this book. The best way to correct these common errors is through the daily grammar lessons—in this way, the students realize that these forms of expression are inappropriate because they are *structurally incorrect.* They should never be taught together as a "unit" on usage, but introduced gradually as they arise in the day-to-day lessons.

Index

Absolute structures, 39
  punctuation of, 42

Accent, 40

Active form, 65

Adjectival clauses, 35, 38, 55

Adjectives, 47
  in subject function, 49
  in verb function, 51
  in complement function, 51
  as noun modifiers, 53
  as verb modifiers, 55
  functions of, 69-70
  form of, 106-108
  inflection to show comparison, 106-107
  characteristic suffixes, 107-108
  teaching, 146-147

Adverbial clauses, 35-36, 38, 56

Adverbs, 47
  in subject function, 49
  in verb function, 51
  in complement function, 51
  as noun modifiers, 54
  as verb modifiers, 55
  functions of, 70-71
  form of, 108-111
  inflection to show comparison, 108-109
  characteristic prefix, 109
  characteristic suffixes, 109-110
  teaching, 150

Affixes, 112-120

Apostrophe, 45

Appositives, 36
  punctuation of, 41

Assimilation, 115, 126

Attributive nouns, 32, 53

Auxiliaries, 26, 72
  teaching, 149

Base morphemes, 83

Basic structural patterns, 19-46

Capitalization, 91
  teaching, 145

Case, 78

Clause, 33

Colon, 41-44

Comma, 41-44

Command or request sentences, 24, 40

Comparative forms
  adjectives, 106-107
  adverbs, 108-109

Complement, 8-9, 20-24
  function of, 51-53
  teaching, 142-144

Complex sentences, 38

Compound sentences, 38-39
  compound subject, 38-39
  compound predicate, 38-39
  compound direct object, 39
  compound indirect object, 39
  punctuation of, 42-43

Connectives, 74-76
  in complement function, 52
  as noun modifiers, 53-54

Content words, 47
  functions of, 56-71
  forms of, 83-111

Coordination, 38-39

Coordinators, 43, 75

Dangling modifiers, 36

Dash, 41, 43, 45

Derivational endings, 6

Derivational morphemes, 83

Determiners, 73
  in subject function, 49
  in complement function, 52
  as noun modifiers, 54
  teaching, 145

Direct objects, 21, 23

Exclamation point, 40, 43

Exclamatory sentences, 24, 40-41

Formation of words, 112-120

Functions within sentences, 47-56

Function words, 6, 11, 47-48, 71-81
  in subject function, 49-50
  in verb function, 51
  in complement function, 52
  as noun modifiers, 53-54
  as verb modifiers, 55
  teaching the function words as signal words, 156

Gender, 77-78

Gerund, 48, 65

Graphemes, 5, 122-125
  consonant graphemes, 122-124
  vowel graphemes, 124-125

Headwords, 10, 20
  teaching, 144

Historical grammar, 4-5

Homonyms, 130-131

Indefinite pronouns, 79
  in subject function, 49
  in complement function, 52

Indirect objects, 23

Indirect questions, 40

Inductive method of teaching,
  134-137

Infinitive phrases, 34-35
  in subject function, 49
  in complement function, 52
  as noun modifiers, 54
  as verb modifiers, 56

Infinitives
  form of, 60-61
  functions of, 65-67

Inflectional endings, 6

Inflectional morphemes, 83

Inner complement, 23

Intensifiers, 32, 73-74

Intransitive verbs, 20, 22, 64-65

Italic type, 46

"Janglish" approach to teaching the New Grammar, 152-158

Juncture, 40

Kernel sentences, 8-10
  basic elements, 19-20
  the five patterns, 20-24, 30
  transformations of, 25-39
  teaching the essential elements,
    138-144
  teaching the N-V pattern, 138-142
  teaching the N-V-N pattern, 142-144
  teaching the N-LV-N pattern, 145
  teaching the N-LV-A pattern, 146-147
  teaching the N-V-N-N and N-V-N-A
    pattern, 151
  teaching the expansion of, 152
  teaching by the "Janglish" approach,
    157

Linking verbs, 22
  teaching, 145-146

Literature, its use in teaching the
  New Grammar, 159-162

Mechanics of sentence structure,
  40-46

Misplaced modifiers, 36

Modification, 29-39
  modifying words within sen-
    tences, 31-37
  single-word modifiers, 31-33
  word-group modifiers, 33-37
  modifying kernel sentence pat-
    terns, 37-39
  modifiers in subject function,
    49
  modifiers of nouns, 53-55
  modifiers of verbs, 55-56

Morphemes, 5, 82

Mutation, 5

Negative sentences, 28-29
  teaching, 150
  teaching by the "Janglish"
    approach, 158

New Grammar, 8-13

Noun clauses, 38
  in subject function, 50
  in complement function, 53

Noun modifiers, 31-32, 53-55

Noun phrases, 8, 20
  teaching, 144

Nouns, 47
  in verb function, 50

in complement function, 51
as noun modifiers, 53
as verb modifiers, 55
functions of, 56-59
in subject function, 48, 57
as subjects of subordinate clauses, 57
as subjects of infinitives, 57
as direct objects of verbs, 57
as direct objects of verbals, 57
as indirect objects, 57-58
as objective complements, 58
as linking-verb complements, 58
as objects of prepositions, 58
as appositives, 58
as headwords in absolute structures, 58
as attributive nouns, 53, 58-59
as possessive modifiers, 53, 59
as adverbs, 59
form of, 84-92
formation of the plural, 84-87
formation of the possessive, 87-88
characteristic suffixes, 88-91
capitalization, 91
identification by stress, 91-92
teaching, 141-144

Number, 77

Objective complement, 23

Outer complement, 23

Parentheses, 41, 45

Participial phrases, 34
in subject function, 48
in complement function, 52
as noun modifiers, 54
as verb modifiers, 56

Participles, 65, 67-69
present, 67-69
past, 69

Parts of speech, 2, 3, 6

Passive form, 10, 28, 65
teaching by the "Janglish" approach, 158

Past form, 61-62

Period, 40, 43

Person, 77

Personal pronouns, 76-79
in subject function, 49
in complement function, 52
as noun modifiers, 53
teaching, 145

Phonemes, 5, 122-125
consonant phonemes, 122-124
vowel phonemes, 124-125

Phrase, 33

Pitch, 40

Plurality, 4-5, 6
formation of the noun plural, 84-87
teaching, 147-148

Possession, 6

Possessive case
pronouns, 78-79
nouns, 87-88
teaching, 149-150

Possessive nouns, 53

Predicate, 20
teaching, 139

Predicate verb, 20
function of, 50-51

Prefixes, 83, 113-116
  characteristic verb prefixes, 103-105
  characteristic adverb prefix, 109
  from Latin, 113-114
  from Greek, 114-115

Prepositional phrases, 33-34
  in subject function, 50
  as noun modifiers, 54
  as verb modifiers, 56
  teaching, 151-152

Prepositions, 33, 74-75
  as verb modifiers, 55
  objects of, 48, 58

Present participle form, 62

Pronouns, 76-81

Pronouns used as intensifiers, 79-80

Punctuation, 40-46
  functions of, 40-43
  the punctuation marks, 43-46

Question mark, 40, 43

Question sentences, 25-28, 40-41
  teaching, 151
  teaching by the "Janglish" approach, 157-158

Quotation marks, 42, 45-46

Relative pronouns, 80-81
  in subject function, 50
  as noun modifiers, 53-54

Semicolon, 41-44

Sequential approach to teaching the New Grammar, 137-152

Signal words, 71-72
  teaching the identification of, 156

Singular verb form, 62-63

Spelling, 125-133

Statement sentences, 24, 40

Stress, 40, 91-92
  teaching, 156-157

Structural grammar, 5-8

Structure words, 47-48

Subject, 20
  the subject function, 48-50
  teaching, 141-142

Subordinate clauses, 35-36
  punctuation of, 41
  in subject function, 50
  in complement function, 53
  subordinate adjectival clauses as noun modifiers, 55
  subordinate adverbial clauses as noun modifiers, 56

Subordination, 37-38

Subordinators, 35, 75-76

Suffixes, 6, 83, 118-120
  characteristic noun suffixes, 88-91
  characteristic verb suffixes, 105
  characteristic adjective suffixes, 107-108
  characteristic adverb suffixes, 109-110
  teaching of, 149

teaching by the "Janglish"
approach, 155-156

Syllables, 82

Syntactic levels, 5

Traditional grammar, 1-4

Transforming the kernel sentences,
9-10, 25-39
by rearrangement, 25-28
by introducing new elements, 28-39
teaching, 157-158

Transitive verbs, 21, 64-65

Usage, 164

Uses of sentences, 24-25

Verb modifiers, 32, 55-56

Verb phrases, 8, 20
teaching, 144

Verbal, 32
in subject function, 48
functions of, 65-69

Verbal phrases, 34-35

Verbs, 47
functions of, 59-69
tenses, 60, 63-64
infinitive form, 60-61
past form, 61
present participle form, 62
singular form, 62-63
flexibility of verbs, 63-65
transitive and intransitive verbs,
64-65
the passive form, 65
verb functions apart from predication, 65-69

forms of, 92-105
inflectional changes, 93-103
inflection of regular verbs, 59-60
93-94
inflection of irregular verbs,
94-103
five-part irregular verbs, 96-98
four-part irregular verbs, 98-101
three-part irregular verbs,
101-103
characteristic prefixes, 103-105
characteristic suffixes, 105
identification by stress, 105
teaching, 139-141, 148-149, 152

Word classes, 6, 11, 47-56,
83-112
teaching, 155-157

Word functions, 47-81
teaching, 154-155

Word order, 19, 47
teaching, 153-154

Word roots, 116-118
Latin, 116-117
Greek, 117-118

Words, teaching their
structural characteristics,
155-156
importance of position, 156
importance of stress, 156-157

Writing, its use in teaching the
New Grammar, 162-163

8-1-69
ONBK

OHIO UNIVERSITY LIBRARY

Please return this book as soon as you have finished with it. In order to avoid a fine it must be returned by the latest date stamped below.

		RETURN BY
SEP 2 1969	FEB 8 1975	
OCT 6 1969	JAN 27 1975	JUN 2 1986
JAN 6 1970	JAN 4 1977	
JAN 8 1970	DEC 13 1976	MAY 13 1986
		QUARTER LOAN
JUL 9 1970	SEP 22 1978	JAN 3 1990
	SEP 18 1978	
JUL 22 1970	OCT 2 - 1978	NOV 13 1989
JUN 4 1972	NOV 1 1978	
	OCT 3 1980	QUARTER LOAN
MAY 25 1972	OCT 3 1980	JUN 9 1991
FEB 1 1973	MAY 7 1981	MAY 09 1991
	MAY 8 1981	
AUG 29 1973		
FEB 14 1974	AUG 5 1983	
FEB 7 1974	JUL 18 1983	
MAY 31 1974	FEB 19 1984	
JUN 8 1974	FEB 1 1984	

CF   30M - 2-69